# GEMS OF PRAYERS

### SRI SWAMI SIVANANDA

*Published By*

**THE DIVINE LIFE SOCIETY**
P.O. SHIVANANDANAGAR—249 192
Distt. Tehri-Garhwal, Uttaranchal, Himalayas, India

Price ]   2002   [ Rs. 30/-

First Edition: 1943
Second Edition: 1996
Third Edition: 2002
( 2,000 Copies )

©The Divine Life Trust Society

ISBN 81-7052-124-6

Published by Swami Jivanmuktananda for the Divine Life
Society, Shivanandanagar and printed by him at the
Yoga-Vedanta Forest Academy Press,
P.O. Shivanandanagar, Distt. Tehri-Garhwal,
Uttaranchal, Himalayas, India.

*Om
Dedicated
as a humble offering
to
the struggling Aspirants
in the spiritual path
and the
striving pilgrims on the
way to God-realisation
Om*

"ANANDA KUTIR"
**RIKHIKESH.**

ॐ

17th July 1943.

Beloved aspirants,

There is a mysterious power in prayer. Prayer can work wonders. It can move mountains. It should come from the bottom of your heart with feeling.

Hold on to prayer, no matter how numerous the temptations and difficulties that assail thee may be. Thou shalt build an impregnable fortress by prayer. Prayer is thy refuge and sheet anchor.

Sivananda

# INTRODUCTION

## POWER OF PRAYER

Prayer is the effort of man to commune with the Lord. Prayer is a mighty spiritual force. It is as real as the force of gravity or attraction.

Prayer elevates the mind. It fills the mind with purity. It is associated with the praise of God. It keeps the mind in tune with God. Prayer can reach a realm where reason dares not enter—it can take you to the spiritual Realm or Kingdom of God. It frees the devotee from the fear of death. It brings him nearer to God and makes him feel his essential, immortal and blissful nature.

The power of Prayer is indescribable. Its glory is ineffable. Sincere devotees only realise its usefulness and splendour. It should be done with reverence, faith, *Nishkamya Bhava* (without expectation of fruits) and with a heart wet with devotion. Do not argue about the efficacy of Prayer. You will be deluded. There is no arguing in spiritual matters. Intellect is a finite and frail instrument. Do not trust this intellect. Remove now the darkness of your ignorance through the light of Prayer.

Draupadi prayed fervently; Lord Krishna ran from Dwaraka to relieve her distress. Gajendra prayed ardently; Lord Hari marched with His disc to protect him. It was the Prayer of Prahlada that rendered cool the boiling oil when it was poured over his head. It was the power of Prayer of Mira that converted the bed of nails into a bed of roses; cobra into a flower garland.

When you pray, you are in tune with the Infinite, you link yourself with the inexhaustible cosmic powerhouse of energy *(Hiranyagarbha)* and thus draw power, energy, light and strength from Him.

Prayer does not demand high intelligence or eloquence. God wants your heart when you pray. Even a few words from a humble, pure soul—though illiterate—will appeal to the Lord more than the eloquent, flowing words of an orator or a *Pundit*.

Even when the medical board has pronounced a case to be hopeless, Prayer comes to the rescue and the patient is miraculously cured. There have been many instances of this description. You might know this. Healing by Prayer is really miraculous and mysterious.

He who prays regularly has already started the spiritual journey towards the domain of everlasting peace and perennial joy. That man who does not pray lives in vain.

Prayer has tremendous influence. I have many experiences. If the Prayer is sincere and if it proceeds from the bottom of your heart *(Antarika),* it will at once melt the heart of the Lord.

Do not pray for the attainment of any selfish ends or mundane gifts. Pray for His mercy. Pray for divine light, purity and spiritual guidance. Pray constantly, **"O Lord, let me remember Thee at all times. Let my mind be fixed at Thy lotus feet. Remove my evil habits."**

Prayer generates good spiritual currents and produces tranquillity of the mind. If you pray regularly, your life will be gradually changed and moulded. Prayer must become habitual. If Prayer becomes a habit with you, you will feel as if you cannot live without It.

Prayer can move mountains. Prayer can work miracles. Pray even once from the bottom of your heart: **"O Lord, I am Thine. Thy will be done. Have mercy on me. I am Thy servant. Forgive. Guide. Protect. Enlighten. *Thrahi mam. Prachodayat.*"** Have a meek, receptive attitude of mind. Cultivate *Bhava* in your heart. The prayer is at once heard and responded. Do this in the daily battle of life and realise yourself the high efficacy of Prayer. You must have strong *Astikya Buddhi* (strong conviction in the existence of God).

Do not pray to the Lord with selfish motives. Never pray: "O Lord, let me become rich. Let me have many children, cattle and property. Let my enemies perish. Let me enjoy in heaven for a long time." Never, never pray like this. Never bargain with the Lord. Lord Himself knows all your needs before you think of asking them. He is the Indweller, *Antaryamin*. He feeds and clothes the entire universe. Will He ever forget thee?

Christians have different prayers for getting various gifts and bounties from God. Muslims and all other religionists have daily prayers at sunrise, noon, sunset, just before retiring to bed, and just before taking food. Prayer is the beginning of *Yoga*. Prayer is the first important *Anga* or limb of *Yoga*. Preliminary, spiritual *Sadhana* (spiritual practice) is Prayer.

A *Yogi* can actually visualise, through his inner eye, the dynamic and beneficial effects produced on the mind and body by Prayer. Pray to God unselfishly and sincerely. You will get devotion, purity, light and divine knowledge.

Get up in the early morning and repeat some Prayer. Pray in any manner you like. Become as simple as a child. Open freely the chambers of your heart. Discard cunningness or crookedness. You will get everything. Sincere *Bhaktas* know pretty well about the high efficacy of Prayer. Narada Muni is still praying. Nama Dev prayed and Vittal came out of the image to eat his food. Ekanath prayed and Lord Hari showed His form with four hands. Mira prayed and Lord Krishna served her like a servant. Damaji prayed and Lord Krishna played the part of a menial in paying his dues to the *Badshah*. What more do you want? Pray fervently, right now from this very second.

May you all attain immortality through unselfish and sincere **Prayers** offered to the Lord in the early morning hours! May **Prayer** become part and parcel of your very existence! May the inner eye of intuition be opened in you through **Prayer!!**

Om Santi! Santi!! Santi!!!

Vyasa Pooja, 1943.
Ashadha }
Poornima } 2000. *Sivananda*
17.7.1943.

# CONTENTS

Introduction . . . . . . . . . . v

## Section I

1. Prayer of a Saint . . . . . . . 3
2. Prayer to Gayatri . . . . . . . 4
3. Prayer for Success . . . . . . 5
4. Prayer for Prosperity . . . . . . 6
5. Prayer for an Offspring . . . . . 7
6. Prayer for Averting Accidental Deaths . . 8
7. Prayer for Relief in Scorpion Sting . . 9
8. Prayer for Good Intellect (A & B) . . 10
9. Prayer for All (A & B) . . . . . 12
10. Hindi Prayer . . . . . . . . 14

## Section II

1. Common Prayer—I, II . . . . . 15
2. Prayer for World Peace . . . . . 18
3. Universal Prayer . . . . . . . 20
4. Prayer to Mother . . . . . . . 22
5. Prayer to the Sun . . . . . . . 25
6. Prayer to Panduranga . . . . . . 27
7. Prayer to Lord Krishna—I, II, III . . 28

8. Prayer to Rama—I, II . . . . . . . 32
9. Prayer to Kundalini . . . . . . . 35
10. Prayer of a Bhakta—I, II, III, IV, V, VI . . 37
11. Prayer of a Sadhaka—I, II, III, IV . . . 44
12. Prayer to the Guru . . . . . . . 47
13. Prayer of a Karma Yogin . . . . . . 49
14. Prayer from an Afflicted Soul . . . . 51
15. Prayer of a Vedantin . . . . . . . 53
16. Prayer to the Lord of Kailas—I, II . . . 55
17. Prayer for Health . . . . . . . . 58

## Section III

1. Vedic Prayer . . . . . . . . 60
2. Santi Prayer . . . . . . . . 64
3. Upanishadic Prayer . . . . . . . 66
4. Arjuna's Prayer . . . . . . . . 70
5. Prayer to the Supreme . . . . . . 74
6. Prayer from Anandalahari . . . . . 76
7. Prayer to Lord Siva . . . . . . . 80
8. Prayer from the Puranas . . . . . . 82
9. Prayer from Bhagavata . . . . . . 85
10. Prayer from Ramayana . . . . . . 87
11. Prayer from Mahabharata . . . . . 89
12. Prayer of the Gods . . . . . . . 92
13. Prahlada's Prayer . . . . . . . 95
14. Draupadi's Prayer—I, II . . . . . . 98
15. Devaki's Prayer . . . . . . . . 100

16. Kausalya's Prayer . . . . . . . . . 102
17. Kunti's Prayer . . . . . . . . . 104
18. Prayer of Tulasidas . . . . . . . . 106
19. Prayer of Ramalingaswami . . . . . 107
20. Gauranga's Prayer . . . . . . . . 108
21. Prayer of a Boy . . . . . . . . . 109

## Section IV

1. Prayer of the Hindus . . . . . . . . 111
2. Prayer of the Zoroastrians . . . . . . 113
3. Prayer of the Jains . . . . . . . . 114
4. Prayer of the Hebrews . . . . . . . 116
5. Prayer of the Buddhists . . . . . . . 117
6. Prayer of the Christians . . . . . . . 119
7. Prayer of the Mohammedans . . . . . 121
8. Prayer of the Sikhs . . . . . . . . 122
9. Prayer as per St. Matthews . . . . . 123
10. Gleanings . . . . . . . . . . . 124

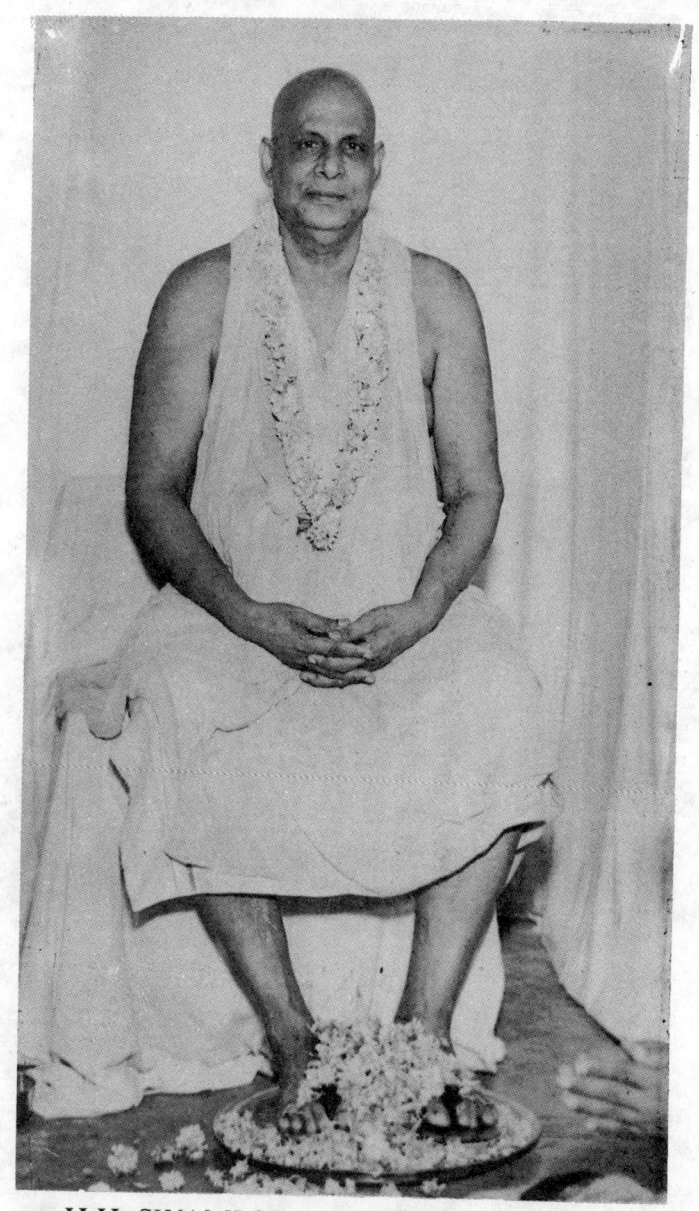
H.H. SWAMI SIVANANDAJI MAHARAJ

# Gems of Prayers

# SECTION I

## 1. PRAYER OF A SAINT

सर्वे भवन्तु सुखिनः
सर्वे सन्तु निरामयाः ।
सर्वे भद्राणि पश्यन्तु
मा कश्चिद् दुःख भाग्भवेत् ॥

May all become happy. Let no one be afflicted by diseases. May everyone come across auspicious things. Let no one be subject to pain, miseries and afflictions.

## 2. PRAYER TO GAYATRI

ॐ

ॐ भूर्भुवः स्वः ॥
तत्सवितुर्वरेण्यं भर्गो देवस्य धीमहि ॥
धियो यो नः प्रचोदयात् ॥

Let us meditate on Isvara and His glory, who has created this universe, who is fit to be worshipped, who is the remover of all sins and ignorance. May He enlighten our intellect!

## 3. PRAYER FOR SUCCESS

ॐ

कृष्ण कृष्ण महायोगिन्
भक्तानामभयंकर ।
गोविन्द परमानन्द
सर्वं मे वशमानय ॥

O Krishna! O Krishna! Thou art the Yogi of Yogis. Thou bestoweth fearlessness on Thy devotees. O Govinda! Thou art the giver of Supreme Bliss. Bring everything in my favour.

## 4. PRAYER FOR PROSPERITY

ॐ

आयुर्देहि धनं देहि
विद्यां देहि महेश्वरि ।
समस्तमखिलं देहि
देहि मे परमेश्वरि ॥

Give me long life, give me wealth, give me knowledge, O Mahesvari—the consort of Mahesvara, Siva. O Paramesvari, give me also everything else that I desire.

## 5. PRAYER FOR AN OFFSPRING

ॐ

देवकी सुत गोविन्द
वासुदेव जगत्पते ।
देहि मे तनयं कृष्ण
त्वामहं शरणं गतः* ॥

O Vaasudeva! O Lord of this Universe! O Son of Devaki! O Govinda! Give me a son, O Krishna! I take refuge in Thee.

* If it is to be recited by the wife it will be गता

---

*Note:* — Repeat one lakh times of this Mantra. Sit for Japa after morning ablutions. After repeating a lakh of times, consult a Pundit and perform Havan. Feed Brahmins, Sadhus and poor, according to your means and distribute clothes and Dakshina.

## 6. PRAYER FOR AVERTING ACCIDENTAL DEATHS

ॐ

ॐ त्र्यंबकं यजामहे
सुगन्धि पुष्टिवर्धनम् ।
उर्वारुकमिव बन्धनान्
मृत्योर्मुक्षीय माऽमृतात् ॥

OM! I bow to that three-eyed Lord Siva, who is full of sweet fragrance, who nourishes the human beings. May He free me from the bondage of Samsara and death, for the sake of Immortality, even as the cucumber is severed from its bondage (of the creeper)

---

*Note:*— Repeat the above prayer 108 times daily. You will be free from accidents and accidental deaths. You will have long life and a healthy body.

## 7. PRAYER FOR RELIEF IN SCORPION STING

ॐ

देवदानव युद्धे
मथ्यमाने महोदधौ ।
जातोऽसि वृश्चिराजस्त्वं
स्वगृहं गच्छ महाविष ॥

In the fight between the Devas and the Demons when the great ocean was churned, O Vrischiraja (king of scorpions), thou emanated from it. Let the great poison of thy sting return to its own abode.

---

*Note:* — Tie a piece of cloth where the pain of the sting is too much. Repeat the above Mantra a number of times. Now untie the cloth and wave it against the air (a gesture to show that the poison has gone down). Continue this routine 8 or 10 times. He who repeats this Mantra at least 108 times a day or who has already attained Mantra Siddhi will be endowed with the gift of cure.

## 8. PRAYER FOR GOOD INTELLECT

—A—

ॐ

य एकोऽवर्णो बहुधा शक्तियोगा-
द्वर्णाननेकान्निहितार्थो दधाति ।
विचैति चान्ते विश्वमादौ च देवः
स नो बुद्ध्या शुभया संयुनक्तु ॥

May that Divine Being, the One who—though Himself colourless—creates various colours in different ways by means of His own power, with set purpose and who dissolves the whole world in Himself in the end—may He endow us with a pure intellect!

*(Svetasvatara Upanishad IV—1)*

– B –

ॐ

यो देवानां प्रभवश्चोद्भवश्च
    विश्वाधिपो रुद्रो महर्षिः ।
हिरण्यगर्भं पश्यत जायमानं
    स नो बुद्ध्या शुभया संयुनक्तु ॥

May Rudra—the Creator and Supporter of the gods—the Great Seer, the Lord of all, who saw Hiranyagarbha being born, endow us with pure (auspicious) intellect.

*(Svetasvatara Upanishad IV–12)*

## 9. PRAYER FOR ALL

### –A–

त्वमेव माता च पिता त्वमेव
त्वमेव बन्धुश्च सखा त्वमेव ।
त्वमेव विद्या द्रविणं त्वमेव
त्वमेव सर्वं मम देवदेव ॥

O Lord! Thou art my Mother and also Thou art my father; Thou art my relative and friend art Thou; Thou art knowledge and wealth unto me; Thou art my All in all, O Lord of lords.

– B –

असतो मा सद्गमय ।
तमसो मा ज्योतिर्गमय ।
मृत्योर्मा अमृतं गमय ॥

O Lord, Lead me from unreal to Real, from darkness to Light, from mortality to Immortality.

## 10. HINDI PRAYER

ॐ

नमो ज्ञान गीता के प्रकाश कर्ता
   नमस्कार अज्ञान के नाश कर्ता ।
नमस्कार बल बुद्धि के देने वाले
   नमो दुःख भक्तों के हर लेने वाले ॥
नमस्ते निराकार सर्व अन्तर्यामी
   नमस्ते परम मित्र सब के स्वामी ।
नमस्ते ज्ञान सागर अविद्या विनाशक
   नमो सच्चिदानन्द घट घट व्यापक ॥
नमो सृष्टि कर्ता तुम ही हो विधाता
   परम सुख मोक्ष का रास्ता दिखाता ।
मुझे दान दो मेरे प्यारे विधाता
   तुम ही प्रभु ईश मुक्ति के दाता ।
विनती प्रभु मेरी स्वीकार कीजो
   बल बुद्धि विद्या हमें दान दीजो ॥

# SECTION II

## 1. COMMON PRAYER

### I

O Omnipresent Lord! Adorations unto Thee. Give me strength to control the mind and to serve Thee and the humanity, untiringly, with great zeal and enthusiasm. Make me a fit instrument for Thy work.

O Loving Presence! Remove my weaknesses, defects and evil thoughts. Make me pure so that I may be able to receive Thy light, grace and blessings.

O Indwelling Presence! Give me a life without disease. Let me remember Thee always. Let me forget the sensual pleasures. Let me have the company of sages and saints. Let me be endowed with dispassion, discrimination and sublime virtues.

O Omniscient Inner Ruler! Prepare me as Thy sweet messenger on this earth so that I may radiate joy, peace and bliss, to the whole world. Let this body, mind and senses, be utilised in Thy service and the service of humanity.

O All-merciful Lord! Let me be conscious of my real divine nature. Let me express my divine nature and divine qualities in my daily actions. Let me become a living presence here.

O Omnipotent Power! Breathe unto me Thy breath of Immortality. Let me drink the divine nectar. Lift me up into the highest realm of supreme peace, eternal bliss and divine splendour. Make me dwell in Thee for ever. Salutations unto Thee. O Lord of compassion!

## II

O Antaryamin, Indweller of our hearts! Friend of the poor, protector of the forsaken, purifier of the fallen (Patitapavana), forgive our sins. Have mercy on us. Show us the smooth way, a royal road for attaining the supreme abode of peace. Open our inner eye of wisdom, the eye of intuition, as Thou once didst for Arjuna—Thy friend and devotee. Throw a flood of light in our spiritual path. Bless us and lighten the load of our mundane life in this Mrityuloka.

O Blessed Lord! All-pervading Truth! Divine effulgence! Remove our hard egoism, lust, wrath, greed, pride, arrogance and Moha (infatuated love for wife, children, property and body or delusion). Cleanse us. Remould us. Make us pure. Give us spiritual strength to attain success in Yoga.

May we surely cross over the ocean of our sin—our terrible enemy—being purified by Thy divine and everlasting grace! When Thy feet shed their grace on man, he gets rid of all his evils—those blessed feet, the threshold of the (noumenal) world, the ever-luminous, the pure, the brilliant, the ever shining and effulgent, that profusely pour their choicest showers of ambrosia in diverse ways on the universe, may they strengthen and consolidate our possession of sound knowledge and righteous conduct on earth.

We bow to Thee, O Indweller of our hearts! Thy teachings constitute the Holy Vedas; nothing can exist without Thee. The whole universe is Thy body. Thou art the light of knowledge. Thou art the supreme Guru, and through Thy grace, may we realise the Truth.

O Lord, the giver of bliss, give us wisdom. Remove all our bad tendencies. Take us under Thy kind shelter so that we may become virtuous. May we all become Brahmacharins and Sadacharins. May we become the protectors of virtue and celibacy.

Salutations to Thee, the Supreme Lord, Thou art the Creator of this universe. Remove the afflictions and miseries of all. Bestow on us the power, courage and strength. Thou art the protector of all beings. Thou art the bestower of peace and bliss. Make everyone happy and cheerful. Thou penetratest all in this universe. Thou cleansest the minds of all impurities. Let us behold the one Self in all. Grant us peace and immortality. May there be welfare to the whole universe. May all devote themselves in doing good to others. May all evil subside. May the world be happy in all ways!

## 2. PRAYER FOR WORLD PEACE

O Adorable Lord! May absolute peace reign over the whole world. May the war come to an end soon. May all nations and communities be united by the bond of pure love. May all enjoy peace and prosperity. May there be deep abiding peace throughout the universe. Grant us eternal peace, the peace that passeth all understanding. May we all work together harmoniously with the spirit of self-sacrifice for the well being of the world. May we all develop cosmic love and universal brotherhood. May we all see God in all faces!

O All-merciful Lord! Grant us an understanding and forgiving heart, broad tolerance and adaptability. O Lord! Grant us the inner eye of wisdom, with which we will behold the Oneness of the Self everywhere.

Peace be to the East. Peace be to the West. Peace be to the North. Peace be to the South. Peace be above. Peace be below. Peace be to all creatures of this universe.

*Sarvesham Svasti Bhavatu*
*Sarvesham Santir Bhavatu*
*Sarvesham Purnam Bhavatu*
*Sarvesham Mangalam Bhavatu.*

May auspiciousness be unto all!
May peace be unto all!
May fullness be unto all!
May prosperity be unto all!

*Lokah Samastha Sukhino Bhavanthu.*

May happiness be unto the whole world!

*OM Poornamadah Poornamidam*
  *Poornath Poornamudachyate*
*Poornasya Poornamadaya*
*Poornamevavasishyate.*

Om! That is full. This is full. From that full this full has come. When this full is taken from that full, it always remains full!

*Om Santi! Santi!! Santi!!!*

Om Peace! Peace!! Peace!!!

## 3. UNIVERSAL PRAYER

O Lord! Thou art the Creator of this universe. Thou art the Protector of this world. Thou art in the grass and the rose. Thou art in the sun and the stars. Salutations unto Thee! O bestower of joy and bliss!

O Sweet Lord! Let me be free from the clutches of death. Let me be able to look upon all beings with equal vision. Let me be free from impurity and sin. Give me strength to control the mind. Give me strength to serve Thee and the humanity untiringly. Make me Thy fit instrument for Thy work. Make me pure and strong.

I bow to Thee, O Indweller of my heart! O Secret of secrets! Remove my weakness, defects and evil thoughts. Make me pure so that I may be able to receive Thy grace and blessings. O Lord! Thou art the thread-soul that connects all beings. Thou pervadest all, permeatest and interpenetratest all things of this universe.

Thou art light divine. Thou art the dispeller of ignorance. Thou art the All-merciful Lord. Give me a life without disease. Let me remember Thee always. Let me develop all sublime virtues.

Thou art self-luminous. Thou art my father, mother, brother, friend, relative and guide. Let me realise the Truth. Let me be free from greed, lust, egoism, jealousy and hatred. Prepare me as Thy sweet messenger on this earth so that I may radiate joy, peace and bliss, to the whole world. Let me utilise this body, mind and senses in Thy service and the service of Thy creatures. Breathe unto me Thy breath of immortality. Let me recognise the universal brotherhood of man. Let me love all as my own Self. Salutations unto Thee, O Lord of compassion!

## 4. PRAYER TO MOTHER

Salutations to the Divine Mother who exists in all beings in the form of intelligence, mercy and beauty. Salutations, O Sweet Mother, the consort of Lord Siva. O Mother Parvati! Thou art Lakshmi. Thou art Sarasvati. Thou art Kaali, Durga and Kundalini. Thou art the embodiment of all power. Thou art Para Sakti. Thou art in the form of all objects. Thou art the sole refuge for all. Thou hast enchanted the whole world. The whole universe is the play of Thy three Gunas. How can I praise Thee? Thy glory is indescribable. Thy splendour is ineffable. Protect me. Guide me, O Loving Mother!

O Adorable Mother! Thou hast generated this great illusion by which all people walk deluded in this world. All sciences have come from Thee. Without Thy grace, no one can get success in spiritual Sadhana and salvation in the end. Thou art the seed for this world. Thou hast two aspects, viz., the unmanifested aspect or Avyaktam and the manifested aspect or the gross universe. The whole world gets dissolved in Avyaktam during Pralaya. Give me the divine eye. Let me behold Thy real majestic form. Help me to cross over this illusion, O Kind Mother!

O Compassionate Mother! I bow to Thee. Thou art my saviour. Thou art my goal. Thou art my sole support. Thou art my guide and the remover of all afflictions, troubles and miseries. Thou art the embodiment of auspiciousness. Thou pervadest the whole universe. The whole universe is filled with Thee. Thou art the storehouse of all qualities. Do Thou protect me. I again and again salute Thee. O Glorious Mother! Salutations to Thee. All women are Thy parts. Mind, egoism, intellect, body, Prana, senses, are Thy forms. Thou art Para Sakti and Apara Prakriti. Thou art electricity, magnetism, force, energy, power and will. All forms are Thy forms only. Reveal to me the mystery of creation. Bestow on me the divine knowledge.

O Loving Mother! Thou art the primal energy. Thou hast two aspects, namely, the terrible and the peaceful. Thou art modesty, gentleness, shyness, generosity, courage, forbearance and patience. Thou art faith in the heart of devotees and generosity in noble people, chivalry in warriors and ferocity in tigers. Give me strength to control the mind and the Indriyas. Make me worthy to dwell in Thee. Salutations unto Thee.

O Mother Supreme! When shall I have equal vision and placid state of mind? When shall I be established in Ahimsa, Satyam and Brahmacharya? When shall I have Thy cosmic vision? When shall I get deep abiding peace and perennial joy? When shall I enter into deep meditation and Samadhi?

O Radiant Mother! I have not done any spiritual Sadhana or service of teachers. I have not practised any Vrata, pilgrimage, charity, Japa and meditation or worship. I have not studied religious scriptures. I have neither discrimination nor dispassion. I have neither purity nor burning desire for liberation. Thou art my sole refuge. Thou art my only support. My silent adorations unto Thee. I am Thy meek suppliant. Remove the veil of ignorance.

O Gracious Mother! Prostrations unto Thee. Where art Thou? Do not forsake me. I am Thy child. Take me to the other shore of fearlessness and joy. When shall I behold Thy lotus feet with my own eyes? Thou art the boundless ocean of mercy. When the philosopher's stone turns iron into gold by contact, when the Ganga turns impure water into pure water, can'st Thou not turn me, O Divine Mother, into a pure soul? May my tongue repeat Thy name always!

## 5. PRAYER TO THE SUN

OM Suryam Sundara Lokanatham Amritam
                    Vedantasaram Sivam,
Jnanam Brahmamayam Suresham Amalam
                    Lokaikachittasvayam,
Indraditya Naradhipam Suragurum Trailokya
                    Chudamanim
Brahma Vishnu Siva Svarupa Hridayam
                    Vande Sada Bhaskaram.

    Om Mitraya Namah
    Om Ravaye Namah
    Om Suryaya Namah
    Om Bhanave Namah
    Om Khagaya Namah
    Om Pushne Namah
    Om Hiranyagarbhaya Namah
    Om Marichaye Namah
    Om Savitre Namah
    Om Arkaya Namah
    Om Adityaya Namah
    Om Bhaskaraya Namah

---

Repeat the above verse and the twelve names of the Sun at sunrise. He who repeats this before the sunrise, early in the morning, will possess wonderful health, vigour and vitality. He will be free from any kind of disease of the eye. He will have wonderful eyesight.

Pray to the Sun in the early morning before sunrise: "O Lord, Suryanarayana, the eye of the world, the eye of the Virat Purusha, give me health, strength, vigour and vitality." Offer Arghya to the Sun in the three Sandhyas (morning, noon and sunset).

Repeat the prayer of the *Isavasya Upanishad*—Slokas 15 and 16. "The face of Truth is covered by a golden vessel. Remove, O Sun, the covering of the law of Truth, that I may behold it. O Pooshan (Sun—nourisher), the only Seer (whole traveller of the heavens), Controller of all (Yama), Surya, son of Prajapati, disperse the rays and gather up Thy burning light; I behold Thy glorious form, I am He, the Purusha within Thee." In the words of the *Yajur Veda*, "O Sun! O Sun of suns! You are All-energy, give me energy; you are All-strength, give me strength; you are All-powerful, give me power."

"I always prostrate before the Sun God,—the beautiful Lord of the world, the immortal, the quintessence of Vedanta, the auspicious, the absolute knowledge, the All-full Brahman, Lord of the Devas, ever pure, the one true consciousness of the world, the Lord of gods and men, the preceptor of Devas, the crest jewel of the three worlds (Bhuh, Bhuvah and Suvah), the form of the heart of Brahma, Vishnu and Siva, the dispeller of darkness and giver of Light."

# 6. PRAYER TO PANDURANGA

Thy name is a boat, Panduranga,
To cross this Samsar, Panduranga,
Thy name is a weapon, Panduranga,
To destroy this Rakshasa-mind, Panduranga.

I am pining for Thy grace, Panduranga,
I am thirsting for Thy mercy, Panduranga,
Reveal Thy true form, Panduranga,
Let me behold It, Panduranga.

Let my mind be fixed, Panduranga,
Always at Thy lotus feet, Panduranga,
Let me utilise this body, Panduranga,
In Thy service always, Panduranga,
This is my fervent prayer, Panduranga,
Do not forsake me, Panduranga.

Thou art everything, Panduranga,
Thou doest everything, Panduranga,
Thou art just, Panduranga,
Thou art Dharma, Panduranga.

Thou art my sole refuge, Panduranga,
Thou art my father-Guru, Panduranga,
Thou art my very Prana, Panduranga,
Thou art my very soul, Panduranga.

## 7. PRAYER TO LORD KRISHNA

### I

Hey Krishna! Thou art my sweet companion now. Thou hast a soft corner for me in Thy heart. Teach me now the mysteries of Thy Lilas and secrets of Vedanta. Thou sayest in the *Gita:* "I am a Vedanta-Krit and Vedavit—I am the author of Vedanta and a knower of Veda." Thou art my best teacher. Explain to me the intricate problems of Vedanta. Give me easy lessons. Kindly explain: Why did Sukha Deva, a Brahma Jnani, who was absorbed in Brahman (Advaita-Samadhi) teach Bhagavata to Parikshit? What are the differences in the experiences of a Bhakta who enjoys the Sayujya state, of a Yogi who is established in Asamprajnata Samadhi and of a Jnani who has Advaita-Avasthanaroopa Samadhi? What is the real difference between Jivanmukti and Videhamukti, Turiya and Turiyatita, Kshara-Purusha and Akshara Purusha and Purushottama?

Let me be frank with Thee, O Krishna, because Thou art the Indweller of my heart, the witness of my mind, and the Lord of my Prana. I cannot hide anything from you because Thou directly witnesseth all the thoughts that emanate from my mind. I have no fear of Thee. Thou art my friend now. Treat me like Arjuna. I shall sing and do Nritya. You can play on the flute. Let us eat together *Makhan Misree*. Let us sing. Teach me Gita. Let me hear it directly from Thy mouth once more.

## II

O Thou Invisible One! O Adorable One! O Supreme! Thou permeatest and penetratest this vast universe, from the unlimited space, down to the tiny blade of grass at my feet. Thou art the basis for all these names and forms. Thou art the apple of my eye, and Prema of my heart, the very life of my life, the very soul of my soul, the illuminator of my intellect and senses, the sweet Anahata music of my heart, and the substance of my physical, mental and causal frames.

I recognise Thee alone as the mighty ruler of this universe and the inner controller of my three bodies. I prostrate again and again before Thee, my Lord! Thou art my sole refuge. I trust Thee alone, O ocean of mercy and love! Elevate. Enlighten. Guide. Protect. Remove all the obstacles from my spiritual path. Remove the veil of ignorance. O Thou Jagadguru! I cannot bear any longer, even for a second, the miseries of this body, this life and this Samsara. Give Darshan quickly. O Prabhu! I am pining, I am melting. Listen, listen, listen to my fervent, Antarika prayer. Do not be cruel, my Lord. Thou art Dinabandhu. Thou art Adhama Uddharaka. Thou art Patita Pavana (purifier of the fallen).

O magnificent Lord of love and compassion! O fountainhead of Bliss and knowledge! Thou art the eye of eyes, the ear of our ears, the Prana of our Pranas, the mind of our minds, and the soul of our souls. Thou art the unseen seer, the unheard hearer, the unthought thinker and the unknown knower. Pray, deliver us from all temptations. Give us light, purity and knowledge.

O Prabhu-Prananatha (Lord of my Prana), Visvanatha, O Vibhu (All-pervading Lord of the universe)! Accept our prayer. Guide us. Lift us from the mire of Samsara. Enlighten us. Protect us. Thee alone we adore, Thee alone we worship, on Thee alone we meditate, in Thee alone we have taken sole refuge.

### III

Oh my Lord! By thinking various useless thoughts, by vain and wild imagination, by entertaining myriads of Sankalpas, my heart and mind are afflicted with severe sores. Enough! Protect me. Oh, do protect me. Turn my thought-current and turn my wandering mind towards Thy lotus feet. Make it rest there for ever. This is my fervent prayer. Give me unswerving, unflinching Ananya Bkakti. This is all I want. Thou knowest my heart already.

Oh, my Lord Krishnaswami, my Antaryami (inner ruler or controller), Avinasi (indestructible), Sarvabhootadhi-vasa (one who abides in all created things), Light of the world, Soul of my soul, life of my life. Relieve me from all temptations. Forgive me. Give me spiritual strength to control my Indriyas and mind. Make me pure. Give me light and knowledge.

Make me a true Brahmachari and Sadachari. Let my mind be ever attached to Thy lotus feet.

Oh, my Lord! I do not want wealth. I do not want beauty. I do not want Kavita Sakti (power to compose poems). I do not want progeny. I do not want name, fame, power or respect. I want Thy Grace, my Hari.

Deprive me of my beauty, wealth, intellectual abilities, house, wife, son, relations and friends, so that my mind may completely be turned towards Thy glorious and effulgent feet. Destroy all the vain pleasure-centres. Do not make me a Pundit. I want to feel Karuna (sympathy) rather to understand its proper definition. If I become a Pundit I will be very far away from Thy feet.

---

*Note:*—The last para is from the viewpoint of a Sadhaka who is endowed with disgust for sensual enjoyments, who wants to entirely dedicate his life for spiritual pursuits, leaving away all attachments and bondage of a worldly life.

## 8. PRAYER TO RAMA

### I

OM, O Beloved Rama! The Indweller of our hearts, (Antaryami). Thou art Satchidananda. Thou art Existence Absolute, Knowledge Absolute and Bliss Absolute. Thou art the Silence of the temple of our hearts. Thou art the effulgence in the Sun, the splendour in the Moon, the glory in the stars, the beauty in the blue sky and the magnanimity in the ocean and Himalayas! Thou art Krishna, Siva, Durga, Parvati, Gayatri and the four Vedas.

We promise to walk in Thy footsteps, ever working, living, moving and breathing in Thee in every second of our lives. We promise to see Thy sweet face in every one, to see Thy glory all round and to recognise Thy presence everywhere and in everything, in trees and flowers, in stones and chairs, in the spring and the autumn.

O Beloved Lord Rama! Ocean of mercy and compassion! Bless us to live in Thy ceaseless flow of light, ever recognising our eternal oneness with Thee from eternity to eternity.

### II

O Ram! In essence Thou art the Light of lights. Thou art the source of everything. Thou art the infinite powerhouse. Thou art the Beauty of beauties. It is Thy effulgent light that lends life and lustre to the Himalayan snowy peaks, sun, moon, stars, flowers and trees, the great scientists, poets, orators, politicians, scholars, philosophers and doctors. Thou art that power which moves the steam-engine, aeroplanes, steamers, railway engines, motor cars, etc. Thou art the beauty at sunset, brilliance in the diamonds, the sweet charming smile in the young maiden, strength in the athletes, endurance in ascetics, intelligence in genii. Above, below, to the right, to the left, in front, behind and everywhere, Thy sweet, effulgent, majestic, magnanimous presence shines.

In the inside of every object there is one Ram alone without any interstice. Wherever I see, there is Ram. Wherever I go, there is Ram. He ever sports in joy. The whole world is His Lila. In the flower, in the tree, in the sky, there is Ram. In the water, in the wood, in the food, there is Ram. In the post, in the wall, there is Ram. In the umbrella, in the pen, in the paper, there is Ram. Here is Ram, there is Ram. There is no world without Ram. This world is filled with Ram. Everything is Ram. How can I describe His unparalleled glory? Victory to Ram. Glory to Ram. Adorations to Ram. Salutations to Ram. Prostrations to Ram.

O All-merciful Lord! I do not want any higher attainments in the spiritual path. I do not want Siddhis. I do not want either Mukti or Self-realisation. Kindly confer on me even a small ray of that magnanimous virtue, Ahimsa. Let not the words I speak hurt a bit the feelings of others. Bless me with this attribute. With that I can slowly climb up to the top of the spiritual ladder like the snail. This is my fervent prayer. O Beloved Ram, have mercy on me. Many a time have I prayed but still my prayer remains unanswered. Perhaps I am still unfit to receive Thy grace. Let me make myself worthy, O Lord of compassion.

O Lord! Through Thy grace may I realise the Truth. May I always entertain sublime thoughts. May I realise myself as the Light Divine. May I be free from greed, lust, egoism, jealousy and hatred. May I serve the humanity with Atma Bhava. May I behold the one sweet immortal Self in all beings. May I realise Brahman with pure understanding.

## 9. PRAYER TO KUNDALINI

O Mother Divine, O serpentine Kundalini Sakti!
Indweller of our hearts,
Thou sleepest in the Muladhara
With three and a half coils.

Thou art unfathomable
Thou art incomprehensible
Thou art unthinkable.
Than art indestructible

Thou art Sakara and Nirakara
Thou art Saguna and Nirguna,
Thou art the source and support,
Thou dwellest in electrons.

Vedas sing of Thee
Sages contemplate on Thee,
Bhaktas worship Thee,
Yogis meditate on Thee.

Let our eyes behold Thee,
Let our hands work for Thee,
Let our tongues praise Thee,
Let our minds be fixed on Thee.

Let us dwell in Sahasrara,
Let our Sushumna be opened,

Let our Kundalini be awakened,
Let us taste the nectar of Hatha Yoga.

Let our Prana be in unison with Apana,
Let us have Kevala Kumbhaka,
Let us attain Samadhi,
Let us become one with Thee.

## 10. PRAYER OF A BHAKTA

### I

Come, come, come, come, O dear Lord, save us, save us, from Mrityu Samsara. Art Thou not an ocean of mercy and love? Hath Thou not saved Dhruva, Prahlada? Art Thou not shining in the chambers of our hearts? Art Thou not glittering in our sparkling eyes? Art Thou not beaming in our glowing faces? Art Thou not throbbing in the beats of our hearts? Art Thou not flowing along the breath in our nose? Art Thou not Sakshi of our wandering minds? Am I not singing Thy name, Ram, Ram, Ram? Am I not chanting Thy name, OM, OM, OM? Am I not working, breathing, and living for Thee, in every second of my life? Am I not feeling Thy presence everywhere? In trees and flowers, stones and chairs, in birds, dogs, in the sun, the moon, and the stars? Now, then, O Lord, fill my heart with Prem.

### II

O Lord! If Thou art the sun, I am the ray; if Thou art the ocean, I am the wave; if Thou art the Himalayas, I am the tree; If Thou art the Ganga, I am the drop; if Thou art the garden, I am the flower; if Thou art the electric light, I am the bulb; if Thou art the landscape, I am the grass. By loving Thee, I have become Immortal; the noose of Yama is cut asunder. Salutations unto Thee.

O Lord! Thou art the Indweller of all; Thou art the soul in all. Thou art the womb of all; Thou art the protector of all. Thou art the bestower of fruits of Karmas to all; Thou art the source of all. Thou art the giver of Moksha to all. Prostrations unto Thee!

O Sovereign Lord of all creations! I do not want any wealth or Moksha or power or dominion. But I do want that the sufferings and troubles of all beings should come to an end for ever. Thou art ocean of mercy. Thou art Omnipotent. Thou canst do this.

O Self-effulgent Lord! Thou art the Supporter, the Saviour, the Creator, the Inner Ruler, the Governor, the Master, the Protector and the Director. Thou art the dispeller of darkness or ignorance. Thou art the remover of the miseries and sufferings of Thy devotees. Thou art the destroyer of the three kinds of Taapas or fevers of human beings.

O Venerable Lord! Salutations unto Thee. In Thee I take refuge. Give me purity and devotion. Let my wandering mischievous mind always rest in Thy blessed Lotus Feet.

O Compassionate Lord! Thou art my father and I am Thy child. Why hast Thou enchained me with these hard fetters? I want to break down the prison of body. I cannot bear the troubles and miseries any longer. Show me Thy smiling face. I wish to hold Thee fast, with both of my arms. Come, come, O my sweet Beloved. Do not delay even a second. I am pining like anything. Thou only knowest the true condition of my heart. Thou alone art my goal and sole refuge. O Lord, save me! Lift me upon Thy bosom. I want nothing else but Thee.

O Lord! The fish cannot live without water. The sunflower cannot live without the sun. The Pativrata cannot live without her husband. The mind cannot live without Prana. The flame of the lamp cannot live without oil. So also I cannot live without Thee; O Lord, enthrone Thyself in my heart. Thou art the Prana of my Pranas. Thou art the Soul of my soul.

## III

O All-pervading, hidden and homogeneous essence! O Adorable Lord of the universe! Thou art witnessing the drama of this world from behind the screen. Thou dwellest in the hearts of all beings. Thou art self-luminous. Thou art the basis for all these names and forms. Thou art one without a second. Thy glory is ineffable. Thou art the source for all sciences, knowledge and beauty.

I do not know how to worship Thee. I have no strength to do any kind of Sadhana. I am full of weaknesses and Doshas. My mind is wavering. Indriyas are powerful and restless. Some say, "Thou art Sakara and Saguna." Others say, "Thou art Nirakara and Nirguna." I do not want to indulge in arguments, discussions and debates. Give me peace and devotion. Give me strength to resist temptations and to control this enemy and thief—mind. Let me utilise my body in Thy service. Let me remember

Thee always. Let me be ever looking at Thy sweet loving face. Grant me this prayer, O Ocean of Love!

Give me true Viveka and lasting Vairagya. The Vairagya cometh and goeth. Let me be established in Para Vairagya. My self-surrender is not perfect and sincere too. I admit my faults. Not a drop of tear comes out of my eyes. Make me weep for Thee, but make me weep in solitude when I am alone. Let me not shed crocodile tears. Then only I can see Thee in my tears. My heart is harder than flint, steel and diamond. How can I make it as soft as butter? Give me the heart of Prahlada and Gauranga. This is my fervent prayer. O Lord of love! Grant me this humble prayer of mine. I am suppliant to Thee. I am Thy disciple. Thou art my Guru.

## IV

O Lord of Brindavan! The joy of Devaki and the refuge of the devotees! Let me repeat Thy names when my Prana leaves my body. Let my Prana leave the body either in Brindavan on the banks of the Yamuna, or in Rishikesh or Benares on the banks of the sacred Ganga. Stand before me, O Lord, with the flute filled with its tune and the crown on Thy head. Let me meditate on this form when my Prana leaves my body. Make me hear Thy melodious flute. Let the Tulasi leaf and Thy Charanamrit be in my mouth. Let the Prana depart with ease. Let me escape from the terrible pain of death. Let no disease torment me when the breath approaches the throat. O Lord of my breath, come to my rescue at that moment. Do not forget this my beloved Krishna. This is my fervent prayer. You will not lose anything if you heed to this. Is this not a part of your duty also? This is my humble request. O All-merciful Lord! Everything is left to Thy choice. Do as it pleases you. I know that you are a Bhaktavatsala, lover of His devotees and Patitapavana, redeemer of the fallen. You are already bound by the string of my love. Certainly, you cannot escape now. Can you, my sweet Beloved?

Come now. Come now. O Flute-bearer! Show Your effulgent face. How shall I entertain Thee, O son of Devaki? Neither milk is there, nor curd, nor butter. Roots do not grow in the earth these days. Fruits and flowers have gone into the hands of others. Deign to accept my humble offering of dry vegetables only. Come, come now, O Lord of the Gopis.

V

O Adorable Lord of compassion! Salutations unto Thee. Give me inner spiritual strength to resist temptation and to melt in Thee this ego, which is harder than granite or diamond. Let me always be Thy chosen playmate in the wonderful game You play in all the worlds. Let me be a perennial channel of Thy sweet love to all Thy children. Utilise my body, the senses and the mind for Thy unhampered play. O hidden love! O sweet silence! O undecaying beauty! Let my soul rest peacefully in Thee for ever and ever.

O Light of lights! O Shining One! I live for Thee. I behold Thee in the smiles of children, in the tears of the afflicted, in my thoughts, emotions, sentiments, in the morning dew of the Himalayan landscape, and in the rays of the sun. My room is filled with Thy sweet presence. I eat Thy benign grace in my daily food. I taste Thy radiant love in my daily drink. Thou art the ocean of love and compassion. Let my love for Thee become a roaring flame. Withdraw from me whatever evil there might be. Fill my heart with purity, goodness, love and sublime virtues. Make me immortal!

O Lord! Reveal unto me Thy enchanting form. Make me feel Thy presence everywhere. Fill my heart with love. Let me merge myself in Thee. Let me walk in the path of righteousness. Cleanse my mind of all evil thoughts. Help me to concentrate my mind on Thy lotus feet. Embrace me and make me pure. Teach me to be still and enjoy Thy magnanimous vision. Illumine my mind with the light of true knowledge. Make my stony heart melt and flow towards Thee.

## VI

O Lord, when will that day come
When I shall see Thee in all?
Give me that eye of wisdom
Which beholds Oneness everywhere.

In this perilous hour I cry unto Thee,
I cannot bear the distress any longer,
Come, come, lift me up, My beloved,
Take me to Thy sweet bosom.

Why are you so cruel, O Lord of Love?
This is not Thy real nature.

Bestow on me Thy grace and mercy,
Abide with me, O friend of the helpless.

Reveal Thy true form to me now,
Do not let me grope in the dark.
Give me light, strength and peace,
O Lord, I sometimes feel Thy gentle touch.

I look to Thee for help and guidance,
Be Thou near and cheer me in my lonely path.
Fill my heart with Thy sweet love,
Make me dwell in Thee for ever and ever.

Just as a Chetak thirsts for the drop of water,
I am thirsting for a drop of Thy grace.
Thou art the ocean of grace and mercy,
Pray do not give me any more trials.

O Lord, in Thee I place my trust,
In Thee I calmly rest.
Thou art All-merciful and Just,
Grant me that, which Thou thinkest best.

Without Thy grace I cannot move,
Without Thy grace I cannot speak,
Without Thy grace I cannot think,
Without Thy grace I cannot live.

## 11. PRAYER OF A SADHAKA

### I

O Loving Lord of the Ocean of Mercy, O Thou Infinite Sea of Serenity! Thou art Varuna, Indra, Brahma, Rudra, Father, Mother, Grandsire, of all. Thou art the blue sky, moon and stars. Hail, hail to Thee, a thousand times. Thou art within, without, above, below, on every side, in front, behind and all-round. Thou art Antaryamin, Witness, and the Lord. Hail unto Thee! Again all Hail!

Thou art all-pervading and interpenetrating; Thou art Sutratman, like the string of a garland; Thou art life, intelligence, thought and consciousness. Bless me to behold Thee everywhere and in everyone. O Sweet Adorable Presence, the Glory of glories, the Sun of suns, Light of lights, Deity of deities! Remove the veil of ignorance that blurs my vision, and grant me strength to realise my Oneness with Thee.

### II

O Lord of Compassion! Hey Prabhu! The Soul of my soul, the Life of my life, the Mind of my mind, the Ear of my ear, Light of lights. Give me light and purity. Let me get established in physical and mental Brahmacharya. Let me be pure in all my thoughts, words and deeds. Give me strength to control my

Indriyas and observe the Brahmacharya Vrata. Protect me from all sorts of temptations of this world. Let all my Indriyas be ever engaged in Thy sweet service. Wipe out the sensual Samskaras and Vasanas. Annihilate the lust from my mind. Make me a true Brahmachari, Sadachari, and an Oordhvareta Yogi. Let me be chaste in my looks. Let me always walk in the path of righteousness. Make me as pure as Bhishma, Hanuman and Lakshman. Forgive all my Aparathams. I am Thine. Guide me. Enlighten my Buddhi!

### III

O Omniscient Lord! Passion is revolting. The Indriyas are turbulent. Mind is skipping like a monkey. Time is fleeting. I do not know what to do. I take Sattvic diet. I practise Pranayama. I do Japa and meditation. Yet passion has not vanished *in toto*. It is suppressed. It is thinned out. But all of a sudden, it bursts out again, like an explosion.

O Adorable Lord! Without Thy grace lust can never be perfectly annihilated. Human exertion alone cannot eradicate this evil trait. Give me strength and energy to control this mischievous imp-mind and the boisterous senses. Give me purity and light. Let me be established in purity. Thou knowest already my heart. I cannot hide my thoughts. Thou art the Antaryami (Inner Ruler) of all, and Silent Witness of all minds.

O All-merciful Lord! Thou art the Ocean of Mercy. If Thou givest me one drop of it, will it dry up the ocean?

## IV

O All-merciful Lord! Time is fleeting. The senses are revolting. The mind is jumping. Maya is deluding. The three fires are burning. The five afflictions are tormenting. Friends are disturbing. Diseases are troubling. Heat of the summer is scorching. Flies, mosquitoes, bugs, scorpions are teasing. The charms of the world are tempting. I can neither concentrate nor meditate. I can do nothing in the spiritual path without Thy benign grace. O Lord! Thou art an Ocean of Mercy. Bless me. If I get a drop from that ocean, will it dry up?

## 12. PRAYER TO THE GURU

O Venerable Guru! Salutations. Thou hast prescribed for me this kind of Sadhana and that kind of practice. I am full of evil qualities. I have committed various evil actions. If my liberation or attainment of God-consciousness depends upon my own exertion, by taking recourse to different practices, where is Thy mercy then? Where is Thy Grace, O Lord? Have mercy on me. I am suppliant to Thee.

May my faith and devotion unto Thee never know decay, even in millions of births, through which I may be doomed to pass, is all what I pray of Thee.

O Lord! Make me dispassionate. O World-teacher! Save me. Remove the veil of ignorance. How long shall I remain in this state of abject ignorance? Give me power to remember Thee always. O Lord! Reveal to me the sublime mysteries of the *Bhagavad Gita*. Reveal to me the secrets of Yoga practice and the method of controlling the mind and the senses. Reveal to me the mysteries of the mysticism in the *Upanishads* and the *Brahma Sutras*. How long shall I fight with these revolting Indriyas?

When will you make me an elevated soul? O Lord! Fill me with magnanimity, generosity, compassion, love, mercy, humility, purity, serenity and adaptability. May nobility and purity follow me wherever I go. May I attain the knowledge of Brahman.

O Lord! Fill my heart with the spirit of Vairagya (dispassion) and humility. Help me in eradicating selfishness, crookedness, lust, anger, greed and jealousy. Let me not hate even my enemies. Make my constricted heart expand like the broad sky.

## 13. PRAYER OF A KARMA YOGIN

O Lord! I do want to serve the world disinterestedly and practise Nishkamya Karma Yoga to get Chitta Suddhi. I am sometimes perplexed, agitated and depressed. I am in a dilemma. I do not know what to do. I have no clear idea of right and wrong. I have no knowledge of the Sastras and the Smritis. I do not know Sanskrit, neither Laghu nor Siddhanta. I have no training to hear Thy shrill inner voice.

This world is full of apparent contradictions, puzzles and paradoxes, troubles and tribulations. This is a peculiar world. Thou hast given me a peculiar mind, with strange habits and ways. Nay, this world is full of temptations. I have no strength to resist temptations, public opinions, criticisms, oppressions, pressure and even aggression. I am not able to please anybody to the fullest extent. Enemies do crop up though I keep quiet, though I do not interfere with anybody.

O Sweet Adorable One! Give me strength to control the restless turbulent Indriyas and the ever-wandering, ever-wavering mind. Stand behind me always and guide me at every step of my action. Give me good Preranas (thoughts). Give me Chitta

Suddhi. Give me a calm, pure and balanced mind. O Lord! Give me light, knowledge and purity.

## OM OM OM

## 14. PRAYER FROM AN AFFLICTED SOUL

I know not the purpose of my life,
I have no idea of Moksha,
I know neither Japa nor meditation,
O Lord! Raise me from this mire of Samsara.

I do not practise mind-control,
I do not know what this mind is,
I have no one-pointedness of mind,
O Lord! Save me from the thraldom of mind.

To whom can I speak out my heart?
Where can I run to find out a shelter?
I am burnt by the three fires,
O Lord! Quench this fire by Thy grace.

I have not served the Sadhus,
I have not done any meritorious act,
I have not fed the poor,
O Lord! Can I also get release in this birth?

I made no Satsanga with the wise,
I did not worship my deity,
I ate, drank, slept and laughed,
O Lord! Can I also expect Thy grace now?

People address Thee as purifier of fallen souls,
There is no credit if Thou savest a virtuous man,

If Thou failest in Thy duty of redeeming a sinner,
O Lord! I will not call Thee Patitapavana.

Thou hast saved Ajamila and Pingala,
Thou hast redeemed Gajendra and Draupadi,
Thou hast helped Dhruva and Prahlada,
O Lord! Why art Thou delaying in delivering me!

My inclination is towards sins,
                      Thy duty is to reclaim me,
I walk my own way, Thou canst walk in Thine.
Pray, keep up Thy prestige and position,
O Lord! Do not lose Thy name Patitapavana.

## 15. PRAYER OF A VEDANTIN

I salute that Supreme Being, Brahman of the Upanishads, by whose commands the earth and the sky do stand apart; by whose commands the sun and the moon always do rotate as the flaming firebrand. I adore Him, by whose commands the seas and oceans do not overstep the limits, and by whose commands the seasons, solstices and the years do not transgress. I ever meditate on that Imperishable Brahman, by whose commands the mind, the Indriyas and the intellect do function properly and keep the life going on.

I bow down to that Brahman which, through its divine powers, though unborn seems to be born, though only one appears to be many, which to the eye of the illusioned appears to be endowed with manifold objective attributes and dispels all the fears of the devotees.

Salutations to that spotless Brahman, who has hidden Himself, like oil in seed, like butter in milk, but who reveals Himself to those who practise constant and intense meditation after purifying their minds by Tapas, continence, right conduct, etc.

My silent adorations to the non-dual, pure, self-effulgent Paramatman, the eternal, all-full, imperishable Brahman, who is the support of my body, mind, Prana and Indriyas, who is the light and substratum of this world, and who is the silent witness of all my mental states and modifications.

## 16. PRAYER TO THE LORD OF KAILAS

I

O Hidden Love and Power that sustains the universe! O Self-luminous light that gives light to my Buddhi (intellect), O Adorable Lord of this universe, Deva of Devas, Lord of lords, Womb of the Vedas, Director (Governor) of the vast universe, Life of my life, Soul of my soul, Prana of my Prana, Mind of minds, Eye of eyes, Ear of ears—ever guide me. Thou art fragrance in the jessamine, beauty in the flowers and the landscape, charm in the skin, Thou art Pranava of the Vedas, the Serene Silence and Peace that dwells in the heart, the Eternal Bliss, the Knowledge that destroys Avidya, (ignorance). Make me always feel the Oneness with Thee.

O Bestower of Purity and Immortality, Thou art the hidden Light of lights that dispels the darkness of nescience, doubt, delusion, the Illimitable Joy that removes pain, grief, sorrow and misery. O Satyam, Jnanam, Anantam, Brahman! O Nityam Amritam, Anadi, Advaitam, Akhanda Satchidananda, the Beauty of beauties, the Spiritual Imperishable Inexhaustible Wealth, the Sweet Honey—purify me. O Thou my dear relative, the inner heart, this body and the indweller, the ovum, the germinal cell, the very life element, the foetus that dwells in the womb of the mother—Thou art everything. O my Kalpa Vriksha that bestows everything—protect me. Let not evil touch me. Let not sins affect me. Purify, elevate and take me to Thy sweet bosom. Make me dwell in Thee for ever.

## II

Let us meditate on Lord Siva, the consort of Parvati, the Lord of lords, the Destroyer of cupid, the Lord of Kailas, the Bestower of knowledge and bliss, the Destroyer of all sins, the Protector of all beings, who holds a trident and Damaru in His hands, and wears a tiger skin around His hips, who is the best among objects of worship, who is full of auspicious qualities, through whose matted hair the Ganga flows.

Adorations to Lord Siva, who is beyond Maya, who is the wielder of Maya, who is the Lord of Yoga, who is capable of being reached through Yoga.

O Lord! If Thou art gracious, a block of stone can give milk. If Thou art gracious, poison will turn into nectar. If Thou art gracious, steel can yield butter. O All-merciful Lord! Have mercy on me. Bestow on me Thy benign grace. Thou art everything. Thou doeth everything. Thou art Just.

O Compassionate Lord! Thou art my father and I am Thy child. Why hast Thou enchained me with these hard fetters? I want to break down this prison of body. I cannot bear the troubles and miseries any longer. Show me Thy smiling face. I wish to hold Thee fast with both of my hands. Come, come, O my sweet Lord. Do not delay even for a second. I am pining for Thy Darshan. Thou only knowest the true condition of my heart. Thou alone art my goal and sole refuge. O Lord, save me, save me. Lift me upon Thy bosom. I want nothing else but Thee.

O Lord! I know not how to pray or do Japa or meditation or mental worship. My heart is quite barren. It is destitute of devotion or good virtues. O Adorable Father! Bless me with Thy magnanimous vision quickly. I cannot bear the pains of Samsara any longer. I am really pining.

## 17. PRAYER FOR HEALTH

O Lord! Bestow on me good health. May I be free from all diseases. Let no disease torment me. Let me continue repeating Thy names always. Let me perform selfless service unto Thy creatures.

Let me go to the abode of immortality, free from all diseases in this very birth. Let my soul be purified by selfless service. Let the fire of repentance burn my physical and mental afflictions.

*Sariramadyam khalu dharmasadhanam*—verily is the declaration of the Sastras. O Lord! Let me not violate the laws of health. Help me in maintaining Brahmacharya by which I may be able to keep up my strength, vigour and energy.

Let me be regular in my physical exercises. Let me perform Yoga Asanas and Pranayama regularly. Let me take moderate and Sattvic diet. O Lord of my Prana! Thou art the witness of my thoughts and actions. Guide me rightly in my daily actions. Let me have pure thoughts. When I sit for food, whisper into my ears the words, **"Be moderate, be Sattvic"** a number of times. As soon as I get up from bed, make me pray unto Thee. Let the strength of my body be utilised in the service of others and not of my own.

With body and mind in healthy condition, let me be able to remember Thee always. Make me healthy so that I may have the capacity to render untiring selfless service and to be regular in my spiritual practices.

O Lord! Help me to reach that Anamaya Pada (state of bliss and immortality) which is entirely free from all diseases, afflictions, cares, worries and anxieties of all kinds.

# SECTION III

## 1. VEDIC PRAYER

In the beginning of creation there was one God, the source of all lights. He was the only Lord of all created beings. He upholds both the earth and heaven. To Him we offer our prayers.

He is the giver of spiritual knowledge. He is the giver of strength. Him all the world worships and by His command all wise men obey. His shelter is immortality. His shadow is death. To Him we shall offer our prayers.

His own greatness has made Him the one sole king of all movable and immovable world. He is the Creator and Lord of all men and beasts. It is to that Lord we shall offer our prayers.

To Thee, O dispeller of all darkness, we offer our prayers with our minds and approach Thee every day, by day and by night.

Let us meditate on the excellent glory of that Divine Being who illumines everything. May He guide our understanding.

*[Rig Veda]*

O Thou Glorious Lord, O Protector of vows, I am determined to master my lower self. Bestow on me the required strength and make my effort fruitful.

Through Thy grace, leaving untruth, may I realise the Truth.

I worship Thee, O sweet Lord of transcendental vision, O giver of prosperity to all! May I be free from the bonds of death, like the ripe fruit falling from the tree. May I never again forget my immortal nature.

O Lord! Who blesses all creatures by revealing the Vedas, deign to make us happy by Thy calm and blissful Self, which roots out terror as well as sin.

Salutations to Thee! O Destroyer of the cycle of births and deaths. O Lord of the universe, adorations to Thee.

O Lord! Thou art beyond the sea of Samsara. Thou existeth in its midst also. Thou enableth one to go beyond sin by means of the sacred Mantras. Thou taketh one beyond death through knowledge. I bow to Thee. Thou art present in sacred flowing streams as well as on the coastland. Thou art in the tender grass on the sea-shore as well as in the foaming waves; I bow to Thee.

May I be able to look upon all creatures with the eye of a friend. May we look upon one another with the eye of a friend.

O Lord! Thou art infinite energy. Do Thou fill me with energy. Thou art infinite virility. Do Thou fill me with virility. Thou art infinite strength. Do Thou bestow on me great strength. Thou art infinite power. Do Thou grant us power. Thou art infinite courage.

Do Thou make me courageous. Thou art infinite fortitude. Do Thou fill me with fortitude.

O Lord! Thou art our father. Do Thou instruct us like a father. Our prostrations unto Thee. Do not forsake us. Do Thou protect us for ever.

Whatever sins have been committed by me, in thought, word, or deed, may the Supreme Lord, the source of all strength, wisdom and purity, forgive me and purify me of them all.

May my body become pure. May I be free from impurity and sin. May I realise myself as the light divine. May my mind become ever pure. May my self become pure. May I realise myself as the light divine.

May we meet together, talk together; let our minds apprehend alike; common be our prayer; common be our assembly's aim; common be our purposes; common be our deliberation; common be our desires; united be our hearts; united be our intention, so that there may be a thorough union among all of us. May our Father grant this.

[*Yajur Veda*]

Let us meditate on the glory and splendour of that Supreme Being, who illumines everything. May He guide us in all our actions. May He grant us a clear understanding and a pure intellect.

Let there be peace in heaven, let there be peace in the atmosphere; may peace fill the four quarters; may the waters and medicinal herbs bring peace; may planets give peace to all beings; may all enlightened persons disseminate peace to all beings; may the Vedas spread peace everywhere; may all other objects everywhere give us peace; and may that peace come to us and remain with us for ever.

[*Yajur Veda* 36—37]

## 2. SANTI PRAYER

He who creates this universe in the beginning, and He whom the Vedas gloriously praise and sing about, in Him I take refuge, in the firm faith and belief, that my intellect may shine with knowledge of Brahman.

Om Santi! Santi! Santi! Om Peace! Peace! Peace!

❋ ❋ ❋

My speech is rooted in my mind, my mind is rooted in my speech; Brahman, reveal Thyself to me! O Ye mind and speech, enable me to grasp the Truth that the scriptures teach. Let that which I have heard slip not from me. I join day with night in study. I think the Truth. I speak the Truth. May That protect me. May That protect the teacher.

Om Santi! Santi! Santi! Om Peace! Peace! Peace!

❋ ❋ ❋

May He, the Lord of all, pre-eminent among the Vedas, and superior to the nectar contained in them, bless me with wisdom. May I be adorned with knowledge of Brahman that leads to Immortality. May my body become strong and vigorous for practising meditation on Brahman. May my tongue always utter delightful words. May I hear a lot with my ears. Thou art the scabbard of Brahman, hidden by worldly taints and not revealed to puny intellects. May I never forget that which I have learnt.

Om Santi! Santi! Santi! Om Peace! Peace! Peace!

⁕ ⁕ ⁕

May the Sun (Mitra) be good to us. May Varuna be good to us. May the Sun Aryama be good to us. May Indra and Brihaspati be good to us. May Vishnu of great strides be good to us. Prostrations to the Brahman. Prostrations to Thee, O Vayu. Thou indeed art the visible Brahman. I shall proclaim Thee visible Brahman. I shall call Thee the Just. I shall call Thee the True. May It protect me.

Om Santi! Santi! Santi! Om Peace! Peace! Peace!

⁕ ⁕ ⁕

May my limbs, speech, Prana, eye, ear, strength and all my senses, grow vigorous. All is Brahman of the Upanishads. May I never deny the Brahman. May the Brahman never spurn me. May there be no denial of the Brahman. May there be no spurning by the Brahman. Let all the virtues recited in the Upanishads repose in me, delighting in the Atman. May they in me repose!

Om Santi! Santi! Santi! Om Peace! Peace! Peace!

## 3. UPANISHADIC PRAYER

The face of Truth is covered by a golden vessel. Remove, O Sun, the covering for the law of the Truth, that I may behold It.

O Pushan (Sun, nourisher), only Seer (sole traveller of the heavens), Controller of all (Yama), Surya, (son of Prajapati), disperse Thy rays and gather up Thy burning light. I behold Thy glorious form. I am He, the Purusha within Thee.

Let my Prana melt into the all-pervading air, the eternal Sutratman and let this body be burnt by fire to ashes. Om! O Mind! Remember, remember, my deeds! O Mind! Remember remember, my deeds!

O Agni! Lead us on to wealth (bliss, Mukti, beatitude) by a good path, as Thou knowest all the ways. Remove the crooked sin from within us. We offer Thee our best salutations.

[*Isavasya Up.* 15 to 18]

As Prajapati, Lord of creatures, Thou movest about in the womb. Thou indeed art born afterwards. To Thee, O Prana, who dwelleth together with the other Pranas (senses), these creatures offer oblations.

Thou art the best carrier to the gods, the first oblation to the forefathers. Thou art the true active principle of the senses (Pranas) which are the essence of the body.

O Prana! Thou art Indra, Thou art Rudra by prowess, Thou art the protector; Thou movest in the sky, Thou art the sun, the Lord of all lights.

When Thou showerest down rain, then, O Prana, these creatures of Thine sit delighted, hoping that there will be food as they desire.

O Prana! Thou art a Vratya (unpurified one), Thou art the fire Ekarshi, the consumer of everything, the good Lord of the world. We are the givers of oblations, O Matarisvan! Thou art our father.

Make propitious that body of Thine which abides in speech, in the ear, in the eye and also which pervades the mind, do not go out.

All this is within the control of Prana, as also all that is in the third heaven. Protect us like a mother. Give us prosperity and wisdom.

[*Prasna Up.* II—7 to 13]

O Rudra! With Thy form which is auspicious, which is not dreadful and which manifests what is holy, with that all-blessed form, appear to us, O dweller among the mountains.

O Lord of the mountains! Make propitious the arrow which Thou holdest in Thy hand to shoot. Do not hurt man or the world, O mountain protector!

[*Svetasva Up.* III—5 to 6]

That itself is Agni (fire), That is Aditya (Sun), That is Vayu (Wind), That is the Chandramas (moon).

That is also the starry firmament. That is the Brahman (Hiranyagrbha). That is water. That is Prajapati.

Thou art the woman, Thou art the man, Thou art the youth, Thou art the maiden too, Thou art the old man who totters along leaning on the staff, Thou art born with Thy face turned everywhere.

Thou art the dark blue fly, Thou art the green parrot with red eyes. Thou art the thunder-cloud, the seasons and the oceans. Thou art without beginning. Thou art the infinite. Thou art He from whom all the worlds are born.

[*Svetasva Up.* IV—2 to 4]

Let us give reverence with oblations to that blissful God, who is the Lord of the Devas, who rules the bipeds and the quadrupeds and in whom all the worlds rest.

[*Svetasva Up.* IV—I3]

O Rudra! Injure not our children, nor our grand children, nor our lives, cows and horses, nor slay in Thy wrath our valiant men. We invoke Thee always with offerings. [*Svetasva Up.* IV—22]

May we know Him, the transcendent and adorable Master of the world, who is the great Supreme Lord of all lords, the Supreme Deity of all deities and the Supreme Ruler of all rulers.

May that only God, who spontaneously covers Himself with the products of Prakriti or nature, just as a spider does with the threads (drawn from its own navel), grant us identity with Brahman.

Let me, desirous of liberation resort to God for refuge whose light turns the intellect, towards the Atman, who at the commencement of creation created Brahma and who gave the Vedas to Him.

[*Svetasva Up.* VI—7, 10, 18.]

Thus purified, without dirt, finally absolved, and free from guilt, may I soar up to the highest heavenly regions, so as to secure equal sojourn with the Almighty Brahman.

O Varuna, I take shelter with Thee, who art fretted with gold, be pleased to bestow upon me, Thy suppliant, purity.

Whatever sin has arisen from my taking food in undesirable places, or from receiving gifts from sinners, and whatever sins have been committed by me in thought, word and deed, all this may Indra, Varuna, Brihaspati, as well as Savitri, remove and purify me again and again.

May death withdraw from us. May immortality approach us. May Vaivasvata (Lord in the sun) vouchsafe us full protection and freedom from all fear. May our wealth develop and increase like the budding leaves of a tree. May Sachipati (Lord of speech) help us.

[*Taitt. Up. Bra.* IV—8, 22 and 65.]

## 4. ARJUNA'S PRAYER

My heart is overpowered by the taint of pity; my mind is confused as to duty. I ask Thee, tell me decisively what is good for me, I am Thy disciple. Instruct me who has taken refuge in Thee.

Thou art the Supreme Brahman, the Supreme Abode, the Supreme Light, the Supreme Purifier, Eternal, Divine Purusha, the Primeval God, Unborn Omnipresent.

All the Rishis have thus declared Thee, O Blessed Lord, neither the Devas nor the Rakshasas know Thy manifestation and origin.

Verily, Thou Thyself knowest Thyself by Thyself O Purushottama, Purusha Supreme, O Source of beings, O Lord of beings, O God of gods, O Ruler of the world.

Thou shouldst indeed tell, without reserve, of Thy divine glories by which Thou existeth pervading all these worlds.

How shall I, ever meditating, know Thee, O Yogin? In what aspects or things, O Blessed Lord, art Thou to be thought of by me?

Tell me in detail, O Janardana, of Thy Yoga powers and glory: for I am never satisfied in hearing Thy life-giving speech.

❖   ❖   ❖

I see all the gods, O God, in Thy body, and also hosts of various classes of beings, Brahma the Lord seated on the lotus, all the Rishis and celestial serpents.

I see Thee of boundless form on every side with manifold arms, stomachs, mouths and eyes; neither the end, nor the middle, nor also the beginning do I see, O Lord of the universe, O Cosmic Form.

I see Thee, with diadem, club and discus; a mass of radiance shining everywhere, very hard to look at, all round blazing like burning fire and sun, and immeasurable.

Thou art the Imperishable, the Supreme Being, worthy to be known. Thou art the great treasure-house of this universe; Thou art the imperishable protector of the eternal Dharma; Thou art the ancient Purusha, I deem.

I see Thee, without beginning, middle or end, infinite in power, of endless arms, the sun and the moon being Thy eyes, the burning fire Thy mouth; heating the whole universe with Thy radiance.

This space between earth and the heavens and all the quarters are filled by Thee alone; having seen this, Thy wonderful and terrible form, the three worlds are trembling with fear, O Great-souled Being.

Verily, into Thee enter these hosts of Devas; some extol Thee in fear with joined palms; "May it be well," thus saying, bands of great Rishis and Siddhas praise Thee with hymns complete.

The Rudras, Adityas, Vasus, Sadhyas, Visveh Devas, the two Asvins, Maruts, Ushmapas and hosts of Gandharvas, Yakshas, Asuras and Siddhas—they are all looking at Thee, all quite astonished.

Having seen Thy immeasurable form—with many mouths and eyes, O mighty-armed, with many arms thighs and feet, with many stomachs and fearful with many teeth—the worlds are terrified and I also.

❂    ❂    ❂

O Hrishikesa! It is meet that the world delights and rejoices in Thy praise; Rakshasas fly in fear to all quarters and all the hosts of Siddhas bow to Thee.

And why should they not, O Great-souled One bow to Thee, greater than all else, the primal cause even of Brahma, O Infinite Being, O Lord of gods, O Abode of the universe, Thou art the Imperishable, the Being and the Non-being, That which is the Supreme which is beyond Sat and Asat.

Thou art the Primal God, the Ancient Purusha, Thou art the Supreme Refuge of this universe, Thou art the Knower, the Knowable and the Supreme Abode. By Thee is the universe pervaded, O Being of infinite forms.

Thou art Vayu, Yama, Agni, Varuna, the moon, Prajapati, and the great grand father; salutations,

salutations unto Thee, a thousand times and again and again salutations, salutations unto Thee.

Salutations to Thee, before and behind! Salutations to Thee on every side. O All, Thou, infinite in power and infinite in prowess, pervadeth all, wherefore Thou art all.

Whatever I have presumptuously said from carelessness or love, addressing Thee as 'O Krishna, O Yadava, O friend', regarding Thee merely as a friend, unknowing of this, Thy greatness.

In whatever way I may have insulted Thee for the sake of fun while at play, reposing, sitting or at meals, when alone with Thee or in company O Achyuta—that I implore Thee, Immeasurable One, to forgive.

Thou art the Father of this world, moving and unmoving. Thou art to be adored by this world. Thou the great Guru; (for) none there exists who is equal to Thee; how can there be then another superior to Thee in the three worlds, O Being of unequalled power?

Therefore, bowing down, prostrating my body, I crave Thy forgiveness, Adorable Lord! As a father forgiveth his son, a friend his friend, a lover his beloved, even so shouldst Thou forgive me, O Deva.

## 5. PRAYER TO THE SUPREME

O Lord Kesava, what I am thinking is this, how am I to please Thee?

The Ganga itself is flowing from Thy feet, shall I take water for Thy ablution then?

Thou hath Satchidananda (Absolute Existence, Consciousness and Bliss), Svarupa (aspects) as Thy cloth. What Pitambara (yellow dress) shall I dress Thee with?

Thou art dwelling in all creatures (animate and inanimate objects) of the universe, O Vasudeva! What Asan shall I give Thee to sit on?

Both the sun and the moon are serving Thee all through, what is the use of showing Thee a looking-glass?

Thou art the Light of all lights. Now tell me what other light shall I burn for Thee?

The Anahata (unceasing eternal sound of OM) is being continued all day and night to welcome Thee. Shall I then play on drums and cymbals or sound a conch to please Thee?

All the four Vedas in all the four speeches (sounds) are singing nothing but Thy praise; what hymns shall I sing for Thee then?

In all Rasas (flavours) there are but Thy flavour only, what other objects shall I place before Thee then as Thy food, Rama?

## 6. PRAYER FROM ANANDALAHARI

Siva is able to create only when He is united with Sakti. Without Her, He (the Deva) will be unable to make a little movement. How can I, unworthy, bow down to Thee or praise Thee, who art worshipped by Hari, Hara, Virinchi and others?

Thou art the effulgent light which dispels the inner darkness (ignorance) of the unwise. Thou art the stream flowing with the honey of consciousness for the ignorant. Thou art the rosary of Chintamani jewels for the poor and the tusk of the boar (incarnated) Muraripu for those who are immersed in the ocean of births and deaths.

All other bands of Devas bestow boons and dispel fear with both their hands; but Mother, O Protectress of the world! Though Thou dost not hold emblems of bestowing a boon or giving shelter, with Thy lotus feet, Thou canst alone protect and grant more gifts than longed for.

O Daughter of the snowy mountain! Great poets like Brahma and the others—great Devas—are not able to imagine Thy beauty. The Devis attain that union with Siva which is not to be attained by austerities, by meditating on Thy beauty.

O Mother! He who contemplates Thee along with Vashini and others—eloquence-givers—brilliant like the moonstone (Chandrakantamani), becomes a great poet whose words, charming in their expression, are sweet with the odour of the lotus-mouth of Sarasvati.

He who, in his heart, contemplates Thee, who diffusest from all parts of Thy body, nectar in the form of rays, as an image carved out of a moonstone, subdues the pride of serpents, like the bird King Garuda and cures those afflicted with fever by his mere look, which sheds cooling nectar.

Eminent men, who with their minds devoid of Maya (impurity and illusion), behold very easily Thy Kala, slender as a flash of lightning, of the essence of the sun, the moon and the fire, placed in the forest of the great lotus above the six lotuses, are immersed in the wave of supreme bliss.

The devotee who wishes to pray to Thee, thus "Oh Bhavani! Mayest Thou cast Thy merciful glance on me Thy servant" and says only "Oh Bhavani mayest Thou...." immediately Thou, whose feet is bowed by the brilliant crowns of Mukunda, Brahma and Indra—bestoweth on him Thine Sayujya state. (Thou doth not wait until the devotee completes his prayer. Thou fulfilleth his desire immediately).

Thou hast got the left half of Sambhu's body and yet Thy mind, I think, is still dissatisfied. It appears that Thou hast taken the other part also, for Thou art now red and three-eyed and slightly bent with the weight of the breasts and Thou art crowned with the crescent moon.

At Thy command, given by a slight motion of Thine eyebrows, Brahma creates the world, Hari sustains it and Rudra destroys it, Isa causes His own form to vanish also and Sadasiva withdraws all objects unto Himself.

O Spouse of Siva! The worship of Thy two feet is the worship of the three Devas (Brahma, Vishnu, and Rudra) born of the three Gunas (Sattva, Rajas and Tamas). These Devas ever stand in obeisance with folded hands on their crowns near the jewelled seat on which Thy feet rest.

O Queen of Chastity! Thy spouse alone exists at the time of the great deluge. Brahma, Hari, Kinasu (Yama), Kubera, die; and even the ever-wakeful eyes of Mahendra (Indra) close (for ever).

O Mother! All the Devas (like) Brahma, Indra, etc., perish though they have drunk the nectar which destroys the fear of the enemies, old age and death. But Siva, who drank even virulent poison, did not die on account of the peculiar greatness of Thy ear-ornaments (Tatanka).

O Mother! May all my speech (and idle talks) be recitation of Mantra; may all actions with my hand be the performing of ritual gesture (Mudra) in Thy worship; may all my eating, etc., be the offering of oblations to Thee; may my lying down be prostration before Thee, may all my pleasures be as dedicating my entire self to Thee. Whatever I do may it be taken for Thy worship.

O Mother! May I, with my six organs as my feet, be as it were, the six-footed (bee) and I seek Thy feet which always give prosperity to the poor, which Thou alone can. Thy feet, lovely like a cluster of Mandara flowers, shed abundant honey of beauty.

O Bhagavati! Thou art the body of Sambhu with the Sun and the Moon as the breasts. I think Thou art the All-pervading stainless One. Hence the relationship as part and whole is the nature common to ye both the same Lordship and the same transcendental bliss.

O youthful Spouse of Siva! Thou art the mind ether, air, fire, water and earth. Thou hast transformed Thyself into the universe and there is nothing beyond. Thou doth manifest Thy consciousness and bliss in the form of the universe by Thy play.

## 7. PRAYER TO LORD SIVA

May Siva, who is pure light and bliss, who is good absolute, protect me everywhere—obeisance to Thee, O Lord, the ever-blissful, the essence of all Truth—fill me with hope; save me from the fear of hell. Endow me with life. Send joy unto my sorrowful mind. Protect me with Thine armour. O Conqueror of Death, Ever-blissful Siva, obeisance to Thee.

Obeisance to Thee, Siva, Teacher of the universe, Giver of bliss, the Yogi of Yogis, Guru of Gurus.

Through misfortune, I am now abased. My mind is filled with sorrow and sin. I am a prey to greed. Delusion and grief possess me. Look on me with merciful eyes, O God, and save me.

My soul Thou art; my mind I liken to Parvati; my Pranas are Thy followers; my body is Thy temple; my enjoyment of things shall be Thy Pooja; my sleep shall be equivalent to meditation on Thee; my wanderings shall form Pradakshina; my words are prayer unto Thee; O Lord, whatsoever I do, consider them all, as worship unto Thee.

In the darkness which encircles me all round and shuts my vision, rise Thou, O Lord, like the Sun and dispel it with Thy light.

Whither shall I fly? What shall I do? How shall I, oppressed with fear, support myself? Why standeth Thou quiet, O Lord, help me, help me, I am fallen at Thy feet?

Siva, Thou art the Lord of the poor; nay their greatest kinsmen; I am the chief among the poor why then speak of our kinship? By Thee alone are to be forgiven all my faults; Thou shouldst actively protect me; for such is the duty of kinsmen.

Ancient hunter! Why wander hither and thither in search of game? There abound, in the wilderness of my mind, all kinds of beasts like jealousy, desire lust, etc.; come kill them and enjoy the sport.

## 8. PRAYER FROM THE PURANAS

Salutations to the supremely effulgent being, who is beyond the great darkness of ignorance. Knowing whom one transcends death. He is the greatest object of knowledge.

Salutations unto Him, whose form is salvation, whom the tranquil-minded men of renunciation attain, having gone beyond merits and demerits and freed from the fear of rebirth.

Nothing is beyond Thy perception, O Lord, but none can perceive Thee. There is nothing which Thou hast not realised and yet Thou art not realised by any.

The sages know Thee to be the primary cause of things, the greatest of all objects. Thou art the ultimate goal of all spiritual attainments. Thou art verily the supreme existence.

Protect me, O Lord of the world. Take pity on me, lover of your devotees. I am helpless and unhappy. I have not attained my goal.

Thou hast pervaded, O Lord, like ether, both within and without this universe. Thou art unattached, immovable, eternal, pure, all-knowing and imperishable.

O Omniscient Lord! Thou art verily the absolute knowledge, the Atman and Master of all beings, the ultimate reality. Thou revealeth unto those who are endowed with knowledge of truth, and who like the bee fix their minds ever on Thy lotus feet.

O Lord, I salute Thee the glorious Being. Thou hath entered into me through Thy own power and roused my dormant faculty of speech. Being the Lord of all powers, Thou enableth me in all my activities with my different organs like hands and feet.

May the world be peaceful. May the wicked become gentle. May all creatures think of their mutual good. May their minds be engaged in good thoughts. And may our hearts be immersed in selfless love for Thee.

Let our speech be engaged in the narration of Thy glory, our ears in hearing Thy wonderful deeds, our hands in serving Thee, the mind in meditation on Thy lotus feet, our heads in prostrations to the entire world—Thy abode—and our eyes to see the righteous who are Thy body.

Whom Brahma, Varuna, Indra, Rudra and the Maruts praise with divine songs; whom Sama-chanters sing with the Vedas and with Angas in Pada and Krama with the Upanishads; whose glimpses (vision) the Yogis get with their minds absorbed in meditation; whose end the gods and demons are ignorant of; to that God all hail!

I prostrate to that Supreme Lord who, dwelling within every being, witnesses the good and bad. Salutations to Him, the All-pervading, the Eternal Witness and Formless.

Salutations to Him, the Omnipresent from whom the universe is inseparable. He, the first cause of the universe, is the one fit object of meditation. May He, the unchanging one, be gracious to us.

O Lord! I do not crave for kingdom, neither heavenly pleasure nor even freedom from births and deaths. May the afflictions of beings, caused by the miseries of life, cease to exist for ever. I pray for this, O my Lord.

Salutations unto Thee, who art free from birth and death. Thou art Death itself. Thou art bright and brilliant like the burning fire itself. Thou art Death to death itself. Adorations to Thee.

## 9. PRAYER FROM BHAGAVATA

Obeisance to that Adorable One, who endows all beings with consciousness, who is the soul of the universe, who constitutes the germ of the universe and who is the Supreme Lord—let us meditate upon Him.

I take refuge in that self-created One, in whom is established this universe, from Whom it had sprung, by whom it had been created, and who Himself constitutes it and who is distinct from cause and effect.

Salutations unto the Highest Lord, unto Brahman, unto Him of infinite power, who is without form, yet with countless forms and unto Him of wondrous works.

Salutations unto Him, who is the light and guide of the soul. He is the witness and Paramatma. Salutations unto the being who is beyond all speech—nay even beyond the reach of mind and the heart.

Salutations unto Him, who is ever peaceful, who is terrific, who is devoid of the senses, who acts in accordance with principles, who is without difference, who is even-natured, who has profound intelligence.

Salutations unto Thee, who art the Supreme Soul, Knower of the field (Kshetrajna), who presides over all, the Witness, the great Purusha, the Origin of all souls and the Source of Prakriti Herself.

Salutations unto Thee, who art the cause of all, who art Thyself the causeless, who doth constitute the wondrous cause of all creation, who art the Vedas and the Agamas; the mighty ocean, the bestower of emancipation and the great refuge of all creatures.

Salutations unto Thee, who severest the halter of ignorance of such humble devoted refugees like me, who art the source of emancipation, the fountainhead of unlimited mercy, who art never idle, who as the inner-soul seated within the hearts of beings, directs their thoughts and actions in accordance with their Karmic law.

Salutations unto Thee, the vigour of whose three divine forces is irresistible, who doth manifest Himself in the form of the objects of sense, the protector of the refugees, of transcendental glory or power, whose way is unattained by those who are bent upon the enjoyment of mundane pleasures.

I bow down unto that Adorable Being, who is difficult of realisation, I, who am not aware of the real nature of my soul, being affected with the energy of His illusion.

[*Gajendra's prayer.*]

## 10. PRAYER FROM RAMAYANA

Thou art, O Raghava, the very Lord Narayana, the glorious being endowed with the invincible weapon discus. Thou art also that indestructible true Brahman, the Supreme Lord, self-existent at all times and in all places in the beginning, in the middle and at the end.

Thou art the embodiment of the highest virtue in all worlds. Thou art the Supreme Being known especially as 'Purushottama' and divine sages proclaim Thee as the worthiest asylum for all, and the saviour of mankind.

Of the three worlds, Thou art the primal Creator and thou art Thyself the self-existent Lord. Thou art the sacrifice, the holy enunciation of the formula 'Vashat' and the sacred syllable 'OM'. Thou art the Highest of the highest.

Thou art seen by the pious and earnest truth-seeker in all creatures, in cows and Brahmins, in the different quarters of the earth, in the sky, as well as in all rivers and mountains.

Thou art the most glorious being; Thou hath a hundred heads, a thousand feet, as well as a thousand eyes, and Thou protecteth the whole earth with all its mountains and all creatures.

Thy teachings constitute the Holy Vedas. Nothing can exist without Thee; and the whole universe is Thy body, Thy energy being the fundamental principle of support of all kinds of existence—animate and inanimate, and our earth being Thyself.

Those devotees, that jealously worship Thee, the Highest Lord, the eternally-glorious Being, will always be duly rewarded, and have their desires fulfilled in this as well as in the other world.

[*Yuddhakanda*]

## 11. PRAYER FROM MAHABHARATA

O Lord, of lotus-like eyes, I, who was till now far away from Thy ennobling and well-meaning influence am now overcome by Thy beauty and grace. Thine is the kingdom, O Lord of the universe! I now find that I am not really my own master, but Thy humble servant. May my obeisance be acceptable unto Thee, O God, the Ruler of all senses and organs. Thou art the Almighty Being and the First of all Existences.

I always seek refuge at Thy feet, the common source of protection for all, whether of the Devas or the Danavas.

Thou art the Sole Creator, Destroyer and the Presiding Deity of the universe. Thou doth permit Thy creatures to act according to their will, Thyself being only a Witness (passive adviser); and Thy nature being veiled by the effects of the three qualities as well as by Maya. Hence Thou art beyond the comprehension of ordinary mortals.

All men, finding in Thee the surest and safest asylum, successfully cross the ocean of Samsara—the vast storehouse of endless pains and sufferings.

Thou hath neither colour, nor shape, nor weapons, nor any particular abode; yet Thou revealeth Thyself unto Thy devotees in some human form.

Nothing is beyond Thy perception, yet Thou art not directly perceived by any. To Thee nothing is impossible of realisation, and none has realised Thee.

The sages know Thee to be the Primary Cause of all effects, the Highest Predicate of all words, and the *summum bonum* or highest good of all Yoga.

O Lord of the Devas! I am terrified at the awful sight of Samsara, the never-ending succession of births and deaths. O Merciful God of lotus-like eyes, protect me with Thy usual grace. I know no other refuge.

Should the natural functions of the body be unfortunately disturbed, by infirmities of age, disease and other ailments, even then I shall always consider myself very fortunate, if my thoughts were centred in Thee; and instead of being lost, they continue to flow in the same direction.

For all the sins of omission and commission, occasioned through ignorance, O Supreme Lord of the Devas, I earnestly beseech Thee to forgive me, considering me as Thy humble and sincere devotee.

Where am I, extremely evil-minded as I am! And where is that thought to seek what is best for me? When such a wide gulf exists between the two, O Madhava, Lord of demigods, kindly Thyself order what is best for me.

The humble services I daily tender to Thee, as in duty bound, in the way of respectful worship and attention to Thee, may actually be an infliction upon Thee, and hence be construed as faults. So I crave Thy pardon, O Lord, the Highest Being, to forgive me for all such misdemeanours.

Lord of the universe! Ever beloved unto Thy votaries with Thy Grace, save me, save me—a helpless, unhappy and unsuccessful creature as I am.

Thou art the Supreme Lord; Thou canst be approached by Thy votaries only through sincere devotion. Thou art the Primal Cause of the universe, its Protector and Destroyer. O Lord of lotus-eyes, the Refuge of the world. I am forlorn and helpless, and know no guide other than Thyself. Take me under Thy care and protection, and save me from all affliction.

[*Yudhishthira's Prayer*]

## 12. PRAYER OF THE GODS

We look upon Thee as our Benefactor. The thought of Thee is the only reality. To attain Thee, truthfulness is the best means. Thou existeth in the three periods of time, the source of the elements, who abides in them as the Indweller, who is the Truth of truth. It is Thou that guideth the operation of true and kind speech and impartiality to all.

The primordial tree of this universe resting on onething—Prakriti—bears two kinds of fruits, happiness and misery. It has three roots Sattva, Rajas and Tamas and four essences, Dharma, Artha, Kama and Moksha. It possesses five attributes of sense organs and six states, viz., birth, growth, etc., seven barks of Dhatus and eight branches (five elements, mind, intellect and ego). It has nine hollows and ten forked leaves (Pranas). Two birds perch upon it—Jiva and Isvara.

O Lord! Thou art the cause for this phenomenal world, Thou art the final resting place for it and Thou art its Protector. Men whose intellect is clouded by Thy Maya, devoid of wisdom, think of Thee as many; but not they who are wise.

Thou Thyself assumeth various forms of pure Sattva for the welfare of the movable and immovable world. Thou art the Atman whose nature is pure consciousness. Thou giveth happiness to the good and chastise the wicked.

Centering their minds on Thee by meditation, the abode of all goodness, some have taken shelter in the boat of Thy lotus feet and easily crossed over this terrible ocean of Samsara finding it as a mere hollow, left by the hoofs of a calf.

Having crossed the fierce ocean of Samsara, those devotees who have unbounded love for Thee, Self-luminous Lord, have left behind, the boat of Thy lotus-like feet. O Lord of Compassion! Thou possesseth unlimited powers, O Lover of Thy devotees.

O Madhava, Thy devotees swerve not from the path, because they have intense love for Thee. Protected by Thee, they move about fearlessly. They place their feet over the heads of the leaders of the army of obstacles and temptations.

Thy name and form cannot be described by enumerating Thy attributes, deeds and births; for Thy ways are only to be inferred and not directly perceived. Thou art the Witness of the mind and speech. Thou art realised by those who engage themselves in the performance of holy acts of contemplation and worship.

O All-powerful Lord! Thou art unborn and causeless. Thou assumeth a human form out of Thy own sweet will and compassion for Thy devotees. Thou art beyond fear. Thou art the Protector and

Guide of all from within. Creation, destruction, and protection, are brought about by Avidya in respect of Thee as Jivatman.

Just as Thou protecteth us always, taking different incarnations like Matsya, Kurma, Narasimha, Varaha and Hamsa, be Thou now pleased to give freedom from fear and protect us and the three worlds and remove the burden of earth. We offer our salutations unto Thee.

## 13. PRAHLADA'S PRAYER

How is it possible for me, born of a cruel race, to praise that Hari whom Brahma and other gods—including Sages and Siddhas—with their mind full of Sattva, are unable even now to propitiate with their streams of prayers, engaged in the praise of His excellent qualities?

I consider that, wealth, high birth, personal beauty, austerities, learning, energy, wisdom and even Yoga practices, are incapable of winning the grace of the Lord Hari who was pleased with the great elephant for its mere devotion.

A Chandala, who has resigned his body, speech, action, wealth and life to the Lord, is far better than a Brahmin—with the twelve favourable conditions—yet averse to the contemplation of the lotus-like feet of Lord Hari. The former purifies the whole of his race but not the Brahmin full of pride.

The Lord, who is ever contented in His own Self, does not crave for the worship offered by little creatures of small intellect. But out of mercy and compassion, He accepts whatever is offered unto Him which turns to his own benefit, just as the decoration or grace added to one's own face is seen reflected in the image on the mirror.

O Absolute Lord, I am not afraid of Thy terrific form with formidable mouth, tongue, eyes shining like the sun, fierce brows, fearful tusks, with a garland of intestines, mane drenched in blood, with ears erect like sticks, the roar that threatens even the protectors of the world, with claws capable of tearing off the hearts of enemies.

But I am afraid, O Friend of the distressed, of the terrible wheel of Samsara, in the midst of which I am placed bound by one's own Karma. O most Adorable Lord, when wilt Thou be gracious enough to call me to Thy presence, the abode of immortality?

I am afflicted in the terrible fire of sorrows of incarnating in various species of beings, through the separation from what is beloved and attainment of what is painful and by failing between the pairs of likes and dislikes, where any remedy for grief is only pain; still ignorant of it, O Perfect Being, I wander about in this Samsara. Be Thou pleased to accept my service and lift me up from this dire Samsara.

Prakriti creates, by Her inscrutable power of Karma (activity), with the help of time under Thy gracious direction, the mind of unmanageable strength inclined to the performance of the Vedic Karmas, which is the wheel of Samsara consisting of the sixteen spokes. O the unborn Lord, how can one without Thy grace, try to attain freedom from it?

Therefore, knowing their nature, I do not crave for these pleasures which the ignorant seek after, viz., long life, wealth, fame, high positions of Indra upto

Brahma even, nor do I wish possession of powers like Anima, etc., which will be snatched away by Thee, O Lord, disguised as Time; keep I pray, me always in the vicinity of Thy servants.

Of what use are the pleasures which are pleasing only to the ears but are unreal like the water in a desert? Of what use is this physical body, the abode of all diseases? Knowing this well, the world never becomes disgusted with it. They try to put out the fire of desires with drops of sensual pleasures.

## 14. DRAUPADI'S PRAYER

### I

O Govinda, O Dweller of Dwaraka, O Krishna, O favourite of the milk-maids, O Kesava, do you not see that I am persecuted by the Kurus? O Lord, O husband of Lakshmi, O Lord of Braja, O Destroyer of all affliction, O Janardana, save me who am sinking in the Kuru ocean!

O Krishna, O Great Yogi, O Soul of the Universe, O Creator of the world, O Govinda, save me who am distressed, who am losing her senses in the midst of the Kurus.

### II

O Krishna, O Krishna, O ye of mighty arms, O Eternal, O Son of Devaki! O Vasudeva, O Lord of the Universe, O ye the killer of the difficulties of those that bow unto you, O Soul of the universe, O Creator of the universe, O Destroyer, O Lord, O Inexhaustible! O the Protector of the afflicted, O the Saviour of kine and subjects, O the Highest of the high, O the Source of the mental perceptions—such as faculties of knowledge and moral sense—I bow to you.

O Worshipful One, O endless Giver of boons, ye the Refuge of the helpless; ye the Ancient, the vital breath, beyond the perception of mental faculties, Oh the Lord of all, the most excellent Lord, I seek Thy refuge; O Lord, O ye fond of Thy votaries, kindly protect me.

O ye having complexion dark as the leaves of the blue lotus, having eyes red as the corola of the lily, O ye clad in yellow garment, O ye adorned with the brilliant Kaustubha, Thou art the beginning and the end of creation; the great Refuge of all, Thou art the Supreme Light and Essence of the universe with your face directed towards all directions. They call Thee the Supreme Germ and the Repository of all Wealth; O King of gods, being protected by Thee, all will lose their terrors. Thou didst save me before from Dussasana in the assembly; it behoves ye now to save me from this difficulty.

## 15. DEVAKI'S PRAYER

O Lord! Thou art in reality the Supreme Lord Vishnu, who illumines the mental substance, whose essence, the sages say, is unmanifest, who is the first cause. Thou art the Perfect Brahman, Intelligence devoid of Gunas and their modifications; attributeless and actionless. Thou art mere existence.

At the close of the period of Brahma, this universe is absorbed into the first and subtle cause and this subtle element also is withdrawn into the unmanifest principle by the velocity of time. Thou alone surviveth with Thy pure consciousness.

I take refuge in Thee, O Lord, O Eternal Ruler of Prakriti! That Time is Thy own sportful activity by which this universe is maintained in its cyclic moving state. Thou art the mighty Time, beginning from the winking of an eye to the life of Brahma! I take refuge in Thee again, who art the abode of bliss and safety.

Being afraid of the serpent of death and roaming about all the worlds, the mortal man fails to find a place free from fear. But, O First Being, by chance by Thy grace, he reaches Thy lotus feet and rests in peace and security. Death flees away from him.

Thou art the Supreme Lord and the One Protector of Thy servants. Protect us who are afraid of the cruel son of Ugrasena. This form of Thine is Supreme in nature and worthy of constant contemplation; pray do not manifest it to the fleshy eyes.

Let not the wicked Kamsa know of Thy birth through me. I am terribly afraid of him for Thy sake. May Thou, O Soul of this universe, withhold this superhuman form from human sight, shining with the brilliance of Sankha, Chakra, Gada and Padma in Thy four arms. Thou art the Supreme Purusha, who holds in Himself this entire universe in its fullest extent during Pralaya. That the Almighty Lord was in my womb is a most wonderful act of ridicule in the world—of men.

## 16. KAUSALYA'S PRAYER

Seeing that Great Lord, Kausalya struck with wonder, with tears of joy running down her eyes, prostrating with folded hands, said:—

O God of gods, O Thou bearer of the conch, the discus and the mace! Salutations unto Thee. Thou art the Supreme Self, the Limitless, Undecaying, Ever Full, the Highest Purusha.

Knowers of the Vedas declare Thee to be beyond speech, intellect and the rest and above the grasp of the senses, of the nature of pure being, with intelligence (Jnana) for Thy form.

Through Thy own Maya Thou alone createth the universe, protecteth it and destroyeth it. Though associated with the attributes of goodness and the rest (passion and darkness), Thou art the fourth, i.e., beyond these three attributes and always pure.

Though doing, Thou art no actor; though going, Thou art really not going. Though hearing, Thou art in reality not hearing; though seeing, Thou art not seeing.

Thou art above Prana, above the mind, pure and so forth, the Vedas have said. Though the same and abiding in all beings, Thou art not cognised as such.

Those whose understandings are deluded by ignorance do not see Thee. Thou art seen by those who are of pure intellect. Worlds are seen to abide in Thy womb like atoms.

That Thou art born of my womb, is only a delusion of the world. Devotion binds Thee to Thy devotees, so I have, O best of Raghus, had a sight of Thee today.

Verily I, who am sunk in this ocean of the world constituted of husband, sons, wealth, etc., and am through Thy Maya wandering in this world, have come today to Thy feet.

O God! Let this form of Thine ever abide in my heart. Let not Thy illusion, which deludes the world affect me.

O Self of the Universe! Do Thou, now withdraw this superhuman form of Thine. Do Thou now show the simple childlike form of delicate and pleasing features.

By pressing that form to my heart, by talking to it in accents of love, I shall go across this great darkness of the Samsara.

## 17. KUNTI'S PRAYER

I adore Thee, the perfect primeval being, the Lord of all, who is above Prakriti, the unperceived, seated within and without every creature.

How can I, an ignorant woman, worship Thee, the Imperishable Being, who art hidden behind the veil of Maya? Just as an actor does not identify himself with the act he plays, even so the ignorant worldly-minded does not perceive Thee?

Thou art hardly seen even by the pure-minded sages, how could then we, women, follow Thy path of devotion and behold Thee?

I bow again and again unto Sri Krishna, Vaasudeva, the joy of Devaki, the beloved darling of Nandagopa and unto Govinda, the Protector of cows.

Prostrations unto Thee who hath the lotus in Thy navel, prostrations unto Thee who wears a garland of lotus flowers, salutations unto Thee with lotus-like eyes and whose feet resemble the beautiful lotuses.

May calamities befall us, now and then, O Teacher of the world! Whereby we shall be blessed with a sight of Thee which causes immortality.

The man whose vision is clouded by the pride of birth, wealth, learning and good fortune is not fit even to praise who art easily attainable by the poor and the sinless.

I bow to Thee, who art the wealth of the poor and who remain unaffected by the three qualities of Maya. I worship Thee, who delight always in Thy own Self, who is Peace and the Lord of Moksha.

Thou art the Kala, the Ruler of all, the One without beginning or end, moving everywhere equally. Unrest is within the elements but there is none in Thee.

No one knows, O Lord, Thy ways, Thou who behaveth like an ordinary man. For Thee there is none dear nor hateful. Different men think differently of Thee.

## 18. PRAYER OF TULASIDAS

Thou art All-merciful, O Lord, and I
       deserve Thy mercy;
Thou art a Donor and I am a poor man;
Thou art the Destroyer of all sins;
       and I am a great sinner;
Thou art the Lord of the helpless and
       there is none so helpless as I;
There is none so afflicted as I and there is
       none else who can relieve my sufferings;
Thou art the Universal Soul and I
       the individual Jiva;
Thou art the Master and I the slave;
Thou art Father, Mother, Teacher, Friend
       and Well-Wisher in every way;
Our relations are in so many diverse ways,
       dispose of me as Thou willeth;
O Compassionate Lord! Tulasidas seeks only shelter
of Thy feet in whatever way it is bestowed on him.

## 19. PRAYER OF RAMALINGASWAMI

O Lord Shanmuga! O Lord Subrahmanya! O Skhanda! Let me have the association of the best wise men who always think of Thy lotus-like feet with one-pointed mind. Let me not have the company of those, who keep one thing inside and talk of another thing—whose thoughts do not agree with their speech. Let me speak always of Thy praise. Let me not utter falsehood. Let me lead a righteous life. Let me not be affected by pride. Let me forget the desire for women. Let me not forget Thee, O Lord! Let me have a pure and auspicious intellect. Let me have the wealth of Thy mercy and grace. Let me live without any disease.

## 20. GAURANGA'S PRAYER

No riches, no retinue, no genius for poetry, O Lord, do I pray Thee for, but may my motiveless devotion to Thee continue in me whenever I incarnate.

Thou hath, O Lord, out of pure compassion and infinite mercy, given to the world a multiplicity of Thy names, made no restrictions whatsoever as to the time, place, etc., for its recitation and bestowed one and all with power and potency, but my ill-luck is such that I lack love for it.

O Son of Nanda! I have fallen headlong into the terrible ocean of Samsara. In Thy mercy consider me as a dust particle of Thy lotus feet so that I may be able to serve Thee as Thy body servant.

O Krishna! When will that blessed time come when, at the utterance of Thy name, my eyes will overflow with tears, my voice will be choked with sobs and the hairs of my body will stand on end.

The separation from you, O Govinda, makes a moment seem to me to be an age, my eyes a thick cloud pouring torrents of rain and the whole world appears to me to be a void.

## 21. PRAYER OF A BOY

### —MORNING PRAYER—

I thank Thee, Lord, for quiet rest,
And for Thy care of me;
O! Let me through this day be blest,
And kept from harm by Thee.

O! Let me love Thee, kind Thou art,
To children such as I;
Give me a gentle, holy heart,
Be Thou my Friend on high.

Help me to please my parents dear,
And do whatever they tell;
Bless all my friends—far and near,
And keep them safe and well.

## —EVENING PRAYER—

Ere on my bed my limbs I lay,
God grant me grace my prayers to say;

O God! Preserve my mother dear
In strength and health for many a year.

And O, preserve my father too,
And may I pay him reverence due.

And may I my best thoughts employ
To be my parents' hope and joy.

And O, preserve my brothers both
From evil doings and from sloth.

And may we always love each other,
Our friends, our father and our mother.

And still, O Lord! To me impart
An innocent and grateful heart.

[*Selected*]

# SECTION IV

## 1. PRAYER OF THE HINDUS

OM! The thousand-headed Purusha, having thousand eyes and thousand feet, Thou pervadeth the whole universe on all sides, and remains over ten fingers. Purusha alone is all this (universe) and which has been and which will be in future. Also He is the Director of Immortality. He is all that which grows out of food. Of this magnitude is His glory and fame, and the Purusha is greater than even this. One-fourth part of His forms all created beings, the immortal or three-fourth parts in the worlds above.

The one Divine Being is hidden in all beings. He pervades all. He is the Inner Self of all beings. He is the Witness of all actions. He dwells in all. He is the Witness, the Consciousness, Independent, Formless and Attributeless.

The One, Self-controlled, who made manifold the one seed from which comes freedom from actions, the self-contented wise who perceive Him in the hearts, for them alone there is eternal happiness and not for the rest.

That blessing do we need, so that we may sing for the sake of sacrifice and for the Lord of sacrifices. May the divine blessing be ours. May the blessing be on our children. May that which is good go always singing unto higher regions. May the blessing be on us, the two-footed as well as the four-footed. Om Peace, Peace, Peace.

Om! O Gods, may we, with our ears hear what is auspicious, O ye! Fit to be worshipped; may we, with our eyes see what is auspicious. May we enjoy the life allotted to us by the gods, offering our praise with our bodies strong of limb. May Indra, the powerful, the ancient of fame, vouchsafe us prosperity. May He, the nourisher and possessor of all wealth, give us what is well for us. May the Lord of swift motion be propitious to us and may the Protector of the great ones protect us too.

## 2. PRAYER OF THE ZOROASTRIANS

Blessed indeed was the thought, blessed the world and blessed the deed of the Holy Zarusthushtra. The celestial Spirits carried forth the scriptures. Glory to you, O Holy Scriptures!

Saluting Thee, O Mazda, we desire Thy gift of gracious help. We stretch our hands unto Thee and pray for the grace of Thy bountiful spirit. We beg of Thee that our actions unto all may be done in the spirit of righteousness and virtue; and with this we may do reverence to the Soul of the Kine.

We remember the Holy Ahunavad Gatha reverentially. He is the Chief of Purity. We reverentially remember His prayer.

We adore the Ha called Yashkaothnem.

We worship the Holy Ahunavad Gatha who is the Lord of Purity. We worship the holy prayer of Ahunavad Gatha. We glorify such men and women whom Ahura Mazda recognises as great in worship and purity.

Purity is the best gift. Happiness is to him who is pure for the sake of purity.

## 3. PRAYER OF THE JAINS

Salutations to the Lord, the Destroyer of enemies, the Supreme Ruler, the King of those who have attained success.

Look with a steady gaze with affection the Lord of the winners, adore the adept in all your actions. Salutation to the Master of him who has reached the other shore of immortality, to the Highest of great eminence, to Him who is above destruction, to Him without any defect. Salutation unto Him who is free from old age, the Immortal, the Wonderful, the Immeasurable Treasure.

Adoration to the Perfect Lord, full of sweetness. I worship His feet with my head with great zeal and enthusiasm, I ever salute Him with folded hands. Salutation to Thee, the Adept, the Illumined, the Good amongst all people in the world, the Shining One, the Joy of all eyes. Salutation to the Chief of all Devas and Asuras and the Great, who serve Him day and night. Adoration to Thee, the Tirthakara, the Bestower of bliss, the Teacher, the Brother who serves without any motive. I adore Thee who longeth for the good of the world, entangled and those who take refuge in Thee, who art the Ocean of the waters of mercy. Salutation to Thee, who art seen in the glass of knowledge, whose nature is both light and darkness.

Salutation to Thee who removeth the taints of all sins and misery, and who driveth away all sense of harassment. Adoration to Thee who art meditated upon by the world as the World Teacher, the Joy of the world, the Lord of the world and of its people. Salutation to Thee who help us to cross the terrible and endless ocean of worldly life, the guide on the way to the City of Bliss. Salutation to Thee, the refuge of the refugeless, unattached, beyond all limitations, formless, the Lord of the world. Salutation to Thee, the enlightener of the meek, the matchless, the Lord of mercy and charity, the pure, the Highest knowledge and the Ruler of the Devas.

## 4. PRAYER OF THE HEBREWS

Hear, O Israel, the Lord is One. The Lord is our God.

May it be Thy will, O Lord and God of our fathers, to make us walk in Thy law and stick to Thy commandments; and lead us away from sin, transgression, temptation and hatred. Remove from us every evil desire and make us adhere to the good.

O Lord, bestow on us Thy grace, favour and mercy in Thy sight and in the sight of all that behold us; and grant gracious favours on us at all times. Glory unto Thee, O Lord, who bestoweth gracious favours on Thy people Israel. Amen.

---

*Note:*—Israel means those who righteously tread the path of God, and in His laws.

## 5. PRAYER OF THE BUDDHISTS

Glory be to the Lord, the Holy Being,
                              perfect in knowledge,
Glory be to the Lord, the Holy Being,
                              perfect in knowledge,
Glory be to the Lord, the Holy Being,
                              perfect in knowledge.

I go to the Buddha (Enlightened) for refuge,
I go to the Law for refuge,
I go to the Brotherhood for refuge.

For the second time, I go to the Buddha for refuge;
For the second time, I go to the Law for refuge;
For the second time, I go to the Brotherhood
                              for refuge.

For the third time, I go to the Buddha for refuge,
For the third time, I go to the Law for refuge.
For the third time, I go to the Brotherhood
                              for refuge.

I promise to abstain from taking the life of
                              any living creature.
I promise to abstain from taking anything
                              with thievish intention.
I promise to abstain from the evil indulgence
                              of bodily passions.

I promise to abstain from falsehood,
I promise to abstain from any
                    intoxicating liquor or drug.

## 6. PRAYER OF THE CHRISTIANS

O Almighty Lord, unto Thee all hearts are open. Unto Thee all desires are known and from Thee nothing is hidden; make pure the thoughts of ours by the inspiration of Thy Holy Spirit, that we may perfectly and wholeheartedly love Thee, and duly glorify Thy Holy Name. Through Christ our Lord. Amen.

O Lord Christ! We, Thy obedient faithful and humble servants, dedicate this newborn day to Thee, praying that it may shine in Thy service as a pure gem in the chaplet of our life. O Thou Great King of love and mercy, Thee we adore and revere ever and for ever. Amen.

To the Most Holy and Adorable Trinity—Father, Son and Holy Spirit—three persons in one God; to Christ, our only Lord and Guide, the Prince of Peace; to the seven mighty spirits before the throne; and to the religious assemblage of just men who have attained perfection, the saints, the holy ones, be unceasing prayer from every living creature; and honour and glory for ever. Amen.

Teach us, O Lord, to see Thy life in all men and in all creatures of Thine earth and guide our nation through its leaders to preserve Thy peace, that the menace of war be far from our country. Through Christ our Lord. Amen.

The peace of God passeth all understanding, keep your hearts and minds in the knowledge and love of God, and of His son, Christ our Lord; and the blessing of God, Almighty the Father, the Son, and the Holy Ghost, be amongst you, and remain with you always. Amen.

## 7. PRAYER OF THE MOHAMMEDANS

In the name of the Lord, the Kind,
                              the Compassionate,
All honour be to God, Lord of all the worlds.
The Kind and the Compassionate, the King
                              on the day of faith.
It is He who is Wise, He who is Powerful.
Guide Thou us on the Path of Righteousness.
The Path of those who rejoice in Thee.
Not on that of those who ignore Thee
                              and work injustice.

        Amin.

## 8. PRAYER OF THE SIKHS

The One Supreme Lord, whose name is the Eternal Truth, the Creator, the Spirit, free from all fear and enmity, Immortal, Birthless, the Self-existent, the Enlightener, the Bestower of Grace. Glory be to Him.

The Pure One was in the beginning, before all ages began; the Pure One exists now, and, says Nanak, shall exist for ever.

Praise be to the Guru!

## 9. PRAYER AS PER ST. MATTHEWS

And when ye pray, ye shall not be as the hypocrites; for they love to stand and pray in the synagogues and in the corners of the streets that they may be seen of men. Verily I say unto you. They have received their reward. But thou when thou prayest, enter into thine inner chamber and having shut thy door, pray to thy Father which is in secret, and thy Father which seeth in secret shall recompense thee. And in praying use not vain repetitions, as the Gentiles do; for they think that they shall be heard for their much speaking. Be not therefore like unto them; for your Father knoweth what things you have need of, before ye ask him. After this manner therefore pray ye: "Our Father which art in heaven, Hallowed be Thy name. Thy kingdom come. Thy will be done, as in heaven, so on earth. Give us this day our daily bread. And forgive us our debts, as we also have forgiven our debtors. And bring us not to temptation but deliver us from the evil one. For Thine is the kingdom and the power and the glory, for ever. Amen." For if ye forgive men their trespasses, your heavenly Father will also forgive you. But if ye forgive not men their trespasses, neither will your Father forgive your trespasses.

## 10. GLEANINGS

Prayer has saved my life. Prayer came out of sheer necessity. I found myself in a plight where I could not possibly be happy without prayer. The more my faith in God increased, the more irresistible became the yearning for prayer. Life seemed to be dull and vacant without it. In fact food for the body is not so necessary as prayer for the soul. For starvation is often necessary in order to keep the body in health, but there is no such thing as prayer starvation. You cannot possibly have a surfeit of prayer. In fact, I have found people envy my peace. That peace comes from prayer.

*Mahatma Gandhi.*

It is the object of prayer and meditation, to shift the centre of consciousness from the lower to the higher, so that "we all, with open face beholding as in a glass the glory of the Lord, are changed into the same image from glory to glory."

The object of prayer is not to attempt to alter the mind, will and purpose of God, but rather to conform our mind to the Divine Mind. Our distress and disharmony are due to the fact that our mind is not conformed to the mind of God.

*Science of Thought Review, London.*

Prayer is not only worship; it is also an invisible emanation of man's worshipping spirit, the most powerful form of energy that one can generate. The influence of prayer on the human mind and body is as demonstrable as that of secreting glands. Its results can be measured in terms of increased physical buoyancy, greater intellectual vigour, moral stamina and a deeper understanding of the realities underlying human relationships. Prayer is a force as real as terrestrial gravity. As a physician, I have seen men, after all other therapy had failed, lifted out of disease and melancholy by the serene effort of prayer.

*Alexis Carrel, M.D.*

Prayer is the pilgrim's staff, the stick in the hand of the mountain climber for averting a fall and promoting an ascent, step by step, towards the highest peak where the shrine of the Deity stands. Prayer gives the surest passport to Heaven. It is the safest route that will lead the aspirant to his destined goal and endow him with the glorious and beatific vision of reality.

*Kalyan Kalpataru.*

Action should be something added to the life of prayer and not something taken away from it. If anyone desires to build a strong edifice which will face the fury of the storm and the dashing of the waves let him know for certain that it must be built on the rock of prayer and not on the loose sand of pelf, power or pedantry.

*Thomas Acquinas.*

Think of God more often than you breathe. In order really to mould personality, prayer must become a habit. It is meaningless to pray in the morning and to live like a barbarian the remainder of the day. True prayer is a way of life; the truest life is literally a way of prayer.

*Epictetus.*

Your prayer is not merely a personal thing with you. It has connection with all people and all spirits. Prayers are substantial creations in the Heaven world. Once prayers are uttered, they travel all over the world through the all-pervading ether. They act upon the great receptive minds, besides vibrating the message upto the seat of God, the very centre of the universe. Remember that the prayer for world peace, being an act of service, will elevate your mind.

*Swami Ramatirtha*

Prayer is the ecstasy of the mystic, the meditation of the sage, and the soaring rapture of the saint.

*Annie Beasant.*

Judge not the Lord by feeble sense,
But trust Him for His grace.

*Longfellow.*

What are men better than sheep or goats,
That nourish a blind life within the brain
If, knowing God, they lift not hands of Prayer
Both for themselves and those who call them
                            friends?

*Tennyson.*

Prayer has tremendous power. It helps the aspirant to realise the hidden divinity. It takes him into the innermost recess of his heart by helping him to pierce through the veil of illusion. It lifts him from the mire of ignorance into the sunshine of knowledge.

*Yoga Sadhana.*

The road of prayer is an ancient road marked by the footprints of pilgrims of many a land and race Prayer is man's intercourse with God, viewed from the human side. It is the language of the spirit which can sometimes be put into words and sometimes not and which, like the language man speaks to man, can only be truly learned and understood as it is practised. In the development of the life of prayer, experience must be at first hand. To pray in His name is in some way to be linked with Him; it is to open the door of our heart to the touch of His spirit. And where the spirit of the Lord is, there is liberty.

*T. Edmund Hillary.*

More things are wrought by prayer than this world dreams of.

*Tennyson.*

Prayer is a power and force that blossoms within the parched up heart, the highest expression of Heavenly illumination. It dispels the dark clouds of nescience and awakening the dormant God-consciousness frees the human soul from its age-old prison into the radiant sunlight of Divinity.

There is no state in the world of existence sweeter than that of prayer. It produces mindfulness, begets the attractions of the Kingdom and engenders the susceptibilities of the Higher intelligence. The supreme attainment of Moses is set forth in the words: "God conversed with Moses."

Prayer is conversation with God. If man concentrates his attention he will, at such times, be aware of the fact that he is indeed in communication with the Divine Power.

Prayer and supplication are so effective that it lifts up the heart and a condition of supreme serenity is realised. Religion without prayer is no religion; for work and worship must go hand in hand, each accentuating to other.

*Abdul Baha*